Talking About
Boys

More Books from A GIRL'S WORLD:

Talking About Friends

Talking About Growing Up

A Girl's World Presents

Talking About
BOYS

Real-Life
Advice from
Girls Like You

Created by A Girl's World Productions, Inc.
www.agirlsworld.com

Edited by Angela Ortiz
With Lynn Barker and Karen Willson

PRIMA GIRLS
An Imprint of Prima Publishing
3000 Lava Ridge Court • Roseville, California 95661
(800) 632-8676 • www.primalifestyles.com

PRIMA GIRLS and colophon are trademarks of Prima Communications Inc. PRIMA PUBLISHING and colophon are trademarks of Prima Communications Inc., registered with the United States Patent and Trademark Office.

All of the characters in this book are based on real persons, but in some cases, names have been omitted or changed to protect the privacy of the people involved. Therefore, any resemblance to actual persons, living or dead, is purely coincidental, unless authorized by the actual person mentioned.

Library of Congress Cataloging-in-Publication Data
Talking about boys : real-life advice from girls like you /
    A Girl's World Productions Inc.
        p.   cm. — (Prima Girls series)
    ISBN 0-7615-3292-7
    1. Teenage girls—Psychology—Juvenile literature 2. Preteens—Psychology—Juvenile literature 3. Teenage boys—Juvenile literature.
4. Interpersonal relations in adolescence—Juvenile literature. I. Girl's World Productions, Inc. II. Series.

HQ798.T33 2001
305.235—dc21   2001021425

01 02 03 04 HH 10 9 8 7 6 5 4 3 2 1

Printed in the United States of America

How to Order
Single copies may be ordered from Prima Publishing, 3000 Lava Ridge Court, Roseville, CA 95661; telephone (800) 632-8676 ext. 4444. Quantity discounts are also available. On your letterhead, include information concerning the intended use of the books and the number of books you wish to purchase.

Visit us online at www.primalifestyles.com

First, with grateful hearts we dedicate this book to God, who in 1996 gave us the idea to go out and build a place on the Internet where what girls think, feel, and do really does matter.

We dedicate this book to the millions of girls who have used their time and talent to share their thoughts, hopes, and dreams with all the other girls of the world at www.a girlsworld.com

With love and peace, we dedicate this book to all our volunteer girl editors (past and present), our AGW Girlcrew, our adult volunteers, advisers, webmaster, family, and friends who made A Girl's World a reality.

Contents

Preface xi
About A Girl's World: What Makes This Book Special xiii
Introduction: Share the Dream xv

CHAPTER 1: GETTING TO KNOW GUYS 1
   I Need Flirting Lessons! 6
   I Really Like a Guy, and I Think He Likes Me,
      But I Don't Know. 8
   My Friend Told This Guy I Like That I Wanted
      to Go Out with Him. 8
   I Don't Have a Boyfriend. How Do I Meet Guys? 9
   The Guy I Like Doesn't Know I Exist. 12
   Homeschooled and Looking for Mr. Right 14
   18 and Not Crushin' on Anybody!
      Can I Ever Catch Up? 16
   He's a Year Older! How Can I Get Things Started? 18
   What If You're Crushing, But You're Too Shy to Do
      Anything About It? 19
   I Attract Jerks and Repel Hotties! 21

CHAPTER 2: WHEN FRIENDS BECOME BOYFRIENDS . . . 27
   Can't a Guy Just Be a Friend?! 27
   Friend or Boyfriend? Where Are We Going? 28
   He's on the Rebound. Do I Tell Him I Like Him? 29
   Lifetime Friends, Until He Hit on Me! 34

My "Friend" Is Calling Me "Babe." Whazzup? 34
My Friends Laugh at My Best Guy Bud! 38
When He Plays Hard to Get 40

CHAPTER 3: CRUSHES **43**
I'm Crushin' on a TV Star! 43
I'm Crushin' on My Male Friend's Relative! 45
I'm Crushin' on an Older Guy. 47
I'm Crushin' on My Best Friend's Older Bro! 50
I'm Going with a Guy, But My Three-Year
    Crush Asked Me Out! 53
He's Pretending to Crush on My Cousin! 54
I've Got a Crush on a "Wolf." Now What? 55
My Best Friend Is the Link to My Crush.
    How Can I Stop Using Her? 57

CHAPTER 4: FAMILY, FRIENDS, AND BOYFRIENDS **61**
The Guy I Like Is My Parents' Worse Nightmare! 61
His Family Doesn't Approve. 62
What Do You Do When Your First Date
    Includes His Little Brother? 63
Not Allowed to Date. I'll Go Nutz! 65
He's Older. Should I Date Him on the Sly? 67
I'm Not Allowed to Talk to Boys on the Phone!
    He Keeps Calling! 72
My Best Friend Dumped Me to Hang with Guys 75
My Friends Think He's Not Good Enough! 77
What Do You Do When You and Your
    Best Friend Like the Same Guy? 80
I Think My Best Friend Lied About
    Me to My Crush! 81
My Best Friend Blabbed to My Crush.
    Now He's Avoiding Me! 83

My Crush's Bud Is a Total Jerk! 87
My B.F. Said Something Insensitive.
   Now My Gal Pals Hate Him! 89

CHAPTER 5: FALLING IN AND OUT OF LOVE 93

First He's Mad, Then Says He Loves Me. Whazzup? . . . 93
First He Stares, Then He Ignores Me. Whazzup? 94
He's Moving On, and I Want Him Back! 95
I Dumped Him. Now I Want Him Back! 97
Memories of a Broken Heart Are Ruining
   My New Relationship. 100
I Love Him, but I'm Starting to Doubt Him. 101
I Was Cold. Now I Think He's a Hottie.
   Should I Tell Him?. 103
How Do You Survive Being Dumped? 105
How Do You Break Up with a Guy?
   I Don't Want to Hurt Him. 106

CHAPTER 6: BOYFRIEND TROUBLE 109

I'm Torn Between Two Guys. 109
Likes Me? Likes Me Not? It's Driving Me Crazy! 110
My B.F. Is Oversensitive and Controlling! 115
He's Older and in College. Should I Go with Him?. . . . 117
My B.F. Is a Dork Fashion Plate!. 118
An Older Boy Got Too "Touchy-Feely." 119
My Guy Is Smothering Me!. 121
When He's with His Pals, I Get the Cold Shoulder!. . . . 126
He "Bad-Mouths" Me to His Friends!. 127
He's My Best Girlfriend's Guy! 128

CHAPTER 7: BOYFRIENDS ON THE INTERNET 129

We Were Online Buds. Now I Want to Be Closer! 129
I Thought I was E-Chatting with My Crush;
   It Was His Friend! 132

He's a Net Chat Romeo, But Does He
Really Like Me? 133
He's Switching Schools! Will We Drift Apart? 136
My Online "Hottie" Went Cold! 137
My Summer Romance Went Home, and I'm Blue! 139

CHAPTER 8: BELIEVE IT OR NOT 143
I Look More Like a "Woman."
Now He's Scared of Me! 143
What Do You Do When You Like Two Brothers? 145
He Prefers TV to Talking with Me! 149
My Cousin Likes a Guy on Drugs. 150
Boys Flirt Then Ignore Me. What Now? 151
Don't Want to Go with Him. 153
Older Guy Leaves Me Cold, But He's My
Bro's Best Friend! 155
My Vacation Romance Followed Me Home! 156
He Thinks I Only Pity Him. 157
All the Girls Are Dissing My Guy Pal! 159

CHAPTER 9: GET IN ON THE FUN! 163
What People Are Saying About Us 163
What Girls Say About AGW 165
What Adults Say About AGW 166
Awards 167
Use the Gold Key Chat Club to Meet New Friends . . . 167
Problems? Get Help! 168
Membership Form 169

Meet the Editor. 171

Preface

My name is Angela Ortiz and I am one of the founding members of A Girl's World Online Clubhouse. Since 1996, our free online magazine has been publishing real life advice and daily, weekly, and monthly features written and edited for girls by girls and teens the world over.

Girls around the world use the Web to come to AGW and submit advice questions to be answered. Our volunteer advice columnists write an answer and send it back to the club to be published weekly. If you have the Web, here's where you can find advice: http://www.agirlsworld.com/info/advice.html

But not every girl has the Internet. So that's where we got the idea to publish this book. We want every girl to get advice from real girls and teens like you!

Talking About Boys is a great book with questions and advice for and by girls about the opposite sex—BOYS!

I am editing this book for many, many reasons. They include the following: I want to help girls understand boys, teach them how to have a great relationship with boys, and how to stay happy and have confidence in finding love. With this book, *Talking About Boys*, I want to do many things for the girls and teens of the world, including not only answering their questions but also giving them advice about their questions and problems.

Girls these days have many problems dealing with boys. Some of these problems include questions like "Does he like me?," "Is he good enough?," "What do I do when I'm too shy to ask him out?," "What do I do when he plays hard to get?," and "What do I do when he's over-possessive?" I think that girls will gain many things by reading this book. They will gain confidence, learn skills, and most of all, read about true experiences that real girls actually had and wrote about for other girls. If you have any questions or comments about this book, you can e-mail me by visiting www.agirlsworld.com. I'd love to hear from you! My penpal number is 181935. I hope you enjoy *Talking About Boys* as much as I do, and I hope you will learn a bunch of stuff about boys. So, take this book, sit down in a comfy chair, and enjoy!

Sincerely,

Angela Ortiz
Girl Editor, A Girl's World Online Clubhouse

About A Girl's World: What Makes This Book Special

"Help me! I'm desperate!" Whether it's dealing with a first crush, family or financial crisis, or peer pressure, pre-teen and teen girls most appreciate advice from their peers. Whatever life throws at a girl, however embarrassing or challenging, another girl has been through it and can help. Is a guy you know totally stressing you out? Girl/Guy relationship driving you crazy? Need advice on how to deal?

Don't bug out, girl! *Talking About Boys* is here to help. On A Girl's World, BoyZone is one of our most popular advice areas. Pre-teens and young teens are just discovering the opposite sex and finding the territory strange and full of potholes and question marks. How can I tell if he likes me? He likes my best friend and I'm jealous. Boys don't know I'm alive. Girls who have already been to that first dance or shared a first kiss can help other girls make that first special moment between a guy and girl less stressful.

The material in this book was written, edited, and suggested by girls and teens. Girls ask the questions and their peers, not grownups, answer them. As members of the adult "Girl's World" team, we had the opportunity to collect, shape, and do a final edit on this book. But what you're holding is truly girl-powered, and that's what makes it special. It was important to our Girlcrew that readers are able to react to what they read here. That's why we hope you enjoy the many opportunities to journal, doodle, talk to your friends, and turn this book into a one-of-a-kind treasure chest you've created that will reflect the experiences of the most important girl in the world—YOU!

Lynn Barker and Karen Willson
Adult Editors, A Girl's World Online Clubhouse

Introduction

Share the Dream

Everything in this book and on our Web site was thought up, planned out, written, and edited by girls and teens the world over. Our mission is to create a space in the world that is entirely girl-powered. We're all about what's possible in a bright future created entirely for and by girls and teens.

After you've read this book, you're invited to get in on the fun. Do you have any stories or advice you'd like to contribute? Your thoughts and opinions really matter to us. Here's how to get in touch or send us submissions for the next *Talking About Boys* book.

Submissions online:
http://www.agirlsworld.com/clubgirl/scoop/index.html

Comments online:
http://www.agirlsworld.com/boytalk.html

Submissions or comments by e-mail:
editor@agirlsworld.com

Subject line:
Talk About: *Talking About Boys* Book

Mailing Address:
A Girl's World Productions, Inc.
ATTN: Talking About Books Editor
825 College Blvd.
PBO 102-442
Oceanside, CA 92057
(760) 414-1092 messages

Getting to Know Guys

First: Who Am I?

Everyone great and small has problems. The first step in solving problems is getting to know your greatest resource: yourself. That means getting to know everything about who you are. The next few pages should help you get started. Fill in as many blanks as you can. Leave anything blank that doesn't apply to you. There are cool places to go to find out some of the answers. Have fun finding out things you don't know!

The only true gift is a portion of yourself.
—Ralph Waldo Emerson
Submitted by
Ellen, 15

MY LIFE!
(A Quick Autobiography of Me)

(Either paste or draw a picture of yourself in the frame, then decorate the cool frame with GELLYZ pens or your fav marker!)

Here's a picture of ME!

Hi! My name is _____.

But I like my friends to call me (nickname)

_____.

Want to know where I got my nickname? Here's what happened:

My favorite exclamation is _____
(like Cool!, Radical!, Far Out!, or whatever)

I am _____ years old.

I was born on (date) _____, which is on this day of the week: _____. (To find out WHICH DAY, go here: http://www.agirlsworld.com /games/jscript/birth-day/birth-day.html)

I was born in (state/country)

_____.

Here's a fun piece of trivia about the state where I was born (To find out WHAT cool U.S. trivia happened in your state, go here: http://www.netstate.com/states/)

Get this! This famous thing happened the same day I was born (To find out WHAT, go to the "History Channel's This Day in History" at this Web site: http://www .historychannel.com/today/)

Did you know? Here's a famous woman who shares my birthday: _____. (To find out WHO, go to the "Women's International Birthday Calendar" at this site: http://www.wic.org /cal/idex_cal.htm)

She's famous because _____

_____.

(continues)

Journalize It!

Here's a picture of my house:

More important, here's my room:

This is what I think about my room. It's totally (description) _____

_____.

Except for the (name it!) _____, of course.

If I had my choice, I'd add this to my room (something you want): _____.

That's because I really want to (what? why?) _____

_____.

If I was a country with a flag, it would look like this:

My proudest moment: The thing I've done so far in my life that I'm the most proud of is this:

Here's a picture of ME doing something cool!

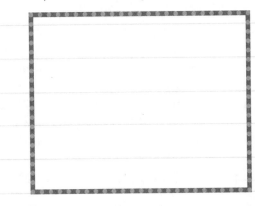

I Need Flirting Lessons!

Dear BoyZone: I would like some advice on how to flirt. I know the basics, but it just seems like they (guys) don't get it. Some girls just run up to the guy and hug them. I think that's a bit much. Others just smile across the room and expect the guy to ask them out. I'd like to do something in between those two extremes. What would you suggest?

—Julia, 13, Canada

WEB watch

CHECK OUT CYRANO!

Want to tell someone how you feel?

Can't find the words? The Cyrano server will help write your love letter!

http://www.nando.net/toys /cyrano.html

A Solution Hey Julia! You're right. Running up and hugging a guy is a lot. Flirting is something you just do most of the time naturally. You might not even realize you're doing it. Flirting is easy. Try to smile, but also talk to him a lot. Guys usually do get it when you flirt with them, but if they have a girlfriend or if they don't like you as a girlfriend, they might not flirt back. If they do like you, they may not respond because they are shy around you. Something in between "hugging" and "smiling" might be to ask one of the guy's friends if he likes you or wait until there's a party or school function and just start chatting with the guy you like. Ask him if he's going and does he want to go together. Good luck!

—Melissa, 13, Massachusetts

To Flirt or Not to Flirt

In most cultures, women are expected to fawn over men, and we usually call that flirting. But do you have to smile or bat your eyelashes to be a flirt? Not at all! Take advantage of a full-length mirror and some time alone. See yourself at a party. Imagine there is someone whose attention you'd like to attract. Look at the way you look, the way you walk, and notice how you feel when you do it. If you are comfortable with yourself, and project the feeling that you find other people interesting, you are the kind of girl people of both sexes will want to talk with. If you are really interested in someone, they almost always enjoy the attention. Be yourself, and you'll be the center of the scene. Write about your experience in front of the mirror— or about a real experience.

I Really Like a Guy, and I Think He Likes Me, but I Don't Know.

The Problem Dear BoyZone: I really like a guy, and I think he likes me, but I don't know. I told him how I feel. He didn't say anything back. What do I do now?

—Lauren, 11

A Solution Hey Lauren! First off he might be a little shocked that you came right out and asked him, so give him about a week or so to come back and tell you his answer. If he doesn't come around then, it might be one of two things: he doesn't like you, or he is really shy. If you think that he is just shy, you will want to be friendly, but back off and let him come around in his own time. You really don't want to put any pressure on him.

—Chastidy, 11, Georgia

My Friend Told This Guy I Like That I Wanted to Go Out with Him.

The Problem Dear BoyZone: My friend told this guy I like that I wanted to go out with him and to kiss him. I'm not even allowed to date!!! And she knows it, too. When I confronted her, she said it was no big deal. It was a big deal to me! What do I do?

—Amanda

A Solution Hey Amanda! That's what happened to me before too. All I did was I told my friend that it embarrassed me, and like a good friend she didn't do it again. Well, with the boy, I just stayed away from him for a while. I waited about two weeks, then I started hanging out with him again (before she told him, I was REALLY good friends with him). It has all worked out perfectly.

—Amber, 11, Michigan

I Don't Have a Boyfriend. How Do I Meet Guys?

The Problem Dear Boy-Zone: I am really desperate because I don't have a boyfriend. I go to an all girl's school. Where can I go to meet guys?

—Frustrated, 14

A Solution Dear Frustrated: I know what it's like not to have a boyfriend and then, to make it worse, not to have any boys around. Here's some ideas about what you could do.

FUNfest

GIFT IDEA: PAPARAZZI PIZZA

Is your special someone in sports? Are you good with a camera? Follow him around with a camera at the next big game. Get that candid shot of him stepping off the team bus, suiting up, sitting on the bench, cheering crowds, the scoreboard, those big moments. Then, develop the pictures and assemble them into a photo collage on a pizza pan. Cover with decoupage. Give the gift of memories. You'll never be forgotten!

—Submitted by Lynn, 12

Speak Out

There are always moments when we wonder if we said the wrong thing or if we should have said anything at all. But unless it's something rude or insulting, it's usually better to express yourself. Use this page, or use your computer, and make a list of five things you've wanted to say.

Example: Tell your teacher she has a great attitude, or thank the bus driver for calling your stop every day, or tell your mom you need some privacy. Now that you have them written out, pick one thing and go say it! Tell 'em what you think, and see what happens!

Maybe if you can get involved in some co-ed sports or get to know some guys through your friends, then you have a chance of getting a boyfriend. There are lots of sports that involve both guys and girls. Some of them are hockey, basketball (even though some aren't co-ed, you're all still a team), soccer, or maybe even just hanging around places where your friends play sports. You can also meet guys through your friends. Like maybe go to the mall one day with one of your friends and have her bring along a few of her guy friends. Maybe even her brothers!

If and when you find a guy you think might be good for you, take things one step at a time. Don't ever just assume that he's great and the perfect one for you when you first meet him. You have to get to know him first. Maybe find out about some of his interests and what he likes to do. Then if you think he likes you and it could work out between you guys, keep in touch with him and give him a few little hints that you like him. Maybe just a "hi" or a little smile every day. Even if you don't find a boyfriend right away, guys are great to have as just friends!

—Chelsea, 12, Nevada

FUNfest

GIFT IDEA: FLOWER POWER!

Here's a bouquet of flowers that never dies! Go to a craft store (or Pic n' Save) and buy a few flowers made of cloth and then tie them in a bow! The flowers usually cost two for a dollar. (You can also get some glue and glitter, dip and decorate the tips of the rose petals for a really sparkling bouquet. Flowers with plastic jewels on them are also really pretty!)

—Submitted by Anny, 11

The Guy I Like Doesn't Know I Exist.

The Problem Dear BoyZone: Help! The guy I like doesn't even know I exist. Now what? Please help me!

—Meg

A Solution Dear Meg: If you like a boy who doesn't know you exist, then why don't you try to get him to notice you? Like, maybe smile at him when he looks at you, or write a note to him or something that might get him to notice you. Then if he starts to look or smile more often at you, he might ask you out. Or if this goes on for a while, then why don't you ask him out? If you're scared, then write a note to ask him if he wants to, and maybe he'll say yes or at least notice you.

—Taryn P., 10, Texas

Another Voice

A Solution Dear Meg: Instead of just worrying what to do, just talk to him a while. Don't worry about trying to figure out what you're going to say. Just act normal. If you don't want to write him a letter or anything, just call him! I have the same problem you do, but I don't mention it or anything. If you want him to know how you feel, tell him by calling, or even writing him a letter. If you don't want to do any of that, just keep quiet until you have the courage to tell him. If you're too shy, and you still can't seem to get any courage, get advice from a friend or talk to someone. So if you don't want to do anything I've listed here, you could have a friend talk to him for you. If they don't want to, don't beg or pay them, just say, okay, well thanks anyway. That's all the advice I have right now, okay? Bye!

—Kara L., 10, Colorado

Q. I like this guy at school, and everyone told me he liked me too, so I asked him out. He said no, and then he never talked to me again! I want to let him know that I still want to be friends. What would you do if this were happening to you?

— Tamara, 13

1 I'd invite him and several other friends to a group activity. But I'd make sure he knew that I wasn't asking him as my date.

Mostly disagree   Somewhat disagree   Somewhat agree   Mostly·agree

2 I'd talk to him when he's alone. I'd explain that it's okay for the two of us to just be friends.

Mostly disagree   Somewhat disagree   Somewhat agree   Mostly agree

3 I'd try to get paired with him on a school project. Then we could work together and have opportunities to talk just as friends.

Mostly disagree   Somewhat disagree   Somewhat agree   Mostly agree

4 I'd forget him. If he won't even talk to me, it's not worth my trouble.

Mostly disagree   Somewhat disagree   Somewhat agree   Mostly agree

Homeschooled and Looking for Mr. Right.

The Problem Dear BoyZone: I really want a new boyfriend. My friends say I should get another one, but I need help with getting one. I'm homeschooled so it's hard for me to meet new boys, and most of the boys that like me aren't attractive to me, and their fathers work for my dad (and if I did make one of them my boyfriend, my dad will kill their dad!). I want the perfect boyfriend but where should I go?

—Heather, 15, USA

A Solution Hey Heather! You want to have the perfect boyfriend? Girl, so does every other girl on this planet! :o) I don't think you should go searching for a boyfriend; enjoy your friends while you can and have fun with your gal pals! You will get a boyfriend when the time is right. Homeschooling can be hard because you don't know as many people. If your friends are telling you to get a boyfriend and you don't really feel that way, maybe you should think about how YOU feel first. You should decide what to do, not your friends.

(*Editor's Note:* If you still want to hook up with a new guy and you are worried about relationships with guys whose dads work for your dad, ask them if they have any friends who might want to go out with you [friends whose dads work elsewhere]. If they ask why you don't go out with them instead, explain that it makes it too awkward and your dad wouldn't like it.

Also, get on the Net with other homeschoolers in your area as pen pals or in chatrooms. If you decide to meet in person someone you met online, be sure you take a parent or go with a group of friends and meet this person in a public place only! Can you go to camp in the summers and meet new friends? There might be someone from your area you didn't know before.)

—Tiffany B., 12, Canada

Q. There's this guy I really like. Somehow I think he got my phone number, and I think he's been calling and hanging up on me. What would you do if this were happening to you?

—Not sure what to think, 10, Tennessee

1 I'd ask my parents if we have a call tracer on our phone line. If we do, then I could use that to find out if he's the one hanging up or not.

Mostly disagree   Somewhat disagree   Somewhat agree   Mostly agree

2 I'd write him a note that just says, "If you've been calling me, stay on the line. I'd like to talk to you."

Mostly disagree   Somewhat disagree   Somewhat agree   Mostly agree

3 I'd just avoid the whole issue by asking him out. If he says yes, then it means he likes me and will probably stop hanging up.

Mostly disagree   Somewhat disagree   Somewhat agree   Mostly agree

4 I'd ask his friends if he's been calling me and hanging up. If they say yes, I'd tell them he should ask me out to a movie or group activity.

Mostly disagree   Somewhat disagree   Somewhat agree   Mostly agree

5 I'd just go right up to him and tell him in person that if he wants to call me, I would like to talk to him.

Mostly disagree   Somewhat disagree   Somewhat agree   Mostly agree

18 and Not Crushin' on Anybody! Can I Ever Catch Up?

The Problem   Dear BoyZone: I'm 18 and I've never ever gone on a date! What should I do? I mean, one of my friends is getting married next month! I've never even had feelings for a guy. Please help me!

—Brenda, 18

A Solution   Hey Brenda! There is no law that says everyone has to get married by a certain age or at all really. I am not saying that you won't get married; I am saying that you shouldn't worry about it. There are a lot of successful and very popular women much older than you who aren't married yet. I'm one of those mushy people who believes there is someone for everyone in this world. Trust me, girl, if there is someone for everyone, then there is one for you, and you will find him, or he will find you. Just hang around guy friends and go out, even if you don't feel attracted to them. "Love" starts with "like," so don't worry about your love life. My parents didn't meet each other until they were in their thirties! You have plenty of time. So go to your friend's wedding, dance with every guy there, and have a blast! You're 18! Your life has just started, like everybody says. Good Luck!

WEB watch

LIKE ADVENTURE? DOES HE?

Unwrap the Mysterious World of Mummies together.

http://www.discovery.com /highspeed/tlc/mummies/

—Lindsay, 14, Louisiana

Q. I'm a tomboy and I hang with the guys a lot. I just found out that they have secretly been fighting about who is going to ask me out. I am really confused. I'm not sure if I like them as more than friends. What would you do if this were happening to you?

—Rose, 14, USA

1 I'd really have to think about it. I'd look hard at my own heart. I must be attracted to one boy more than the others. I'd accept his invitation and see how it goes.

Mostly disagree   Somewhat disagree   Somewhat agree   Mostly agree

2 I'd confront them and tell them to stop thinking of me as more than a friend.

Mostly disagree   Somewhat disagree   Somewhat agree   Mostly agree

3 If they are crazy enough to fight over me, let them. Then I'd go out with the winner.

Mostly disagree   Somewhat disagree   Somewhat agree   Mostly agree

4 I'd start going out with a guy outside our circle of friends. That would get the message across.

Mostly disagree   Somewhat disagree   Somewhat agree   Mostly agree

5 I'd take charge and ask one of them out. Then I'd see how I felt about them after a date.

Mostly disagree   Somewhat disagree   Somewhat agree   Mostly agree

He's a Year Older!
How Can I Get Things Started?

The Problem   Dear BoyZone: There's a boy that I fancy and he's in the year above me. My mum's flat mate asked him if he wants to join me, her, my mum, and brother to go out somewhere "one day," and he said yes. But this boy is very good-looking and polite to everyone, and I want to go out with him before anyone else snaps him up. How can I hurry things along?

—Lesley, 12

A Solution   Hey Lesley! To have a relationship with any boy, it takes hard work, compromising, and patience. Remember, love takes time. You can't force a boy to like you and hurry things. You should take a step at a time, very steady so you won't lose your balance. He probably won't want to talk to you in the hallways or after school, because the boys in his class might think he's "uncool" if he's talking to a girl younger than him. But try calling him if you have his phone number. When you bump into him, act casual and not too "into it." He might think you're some kind of psycho. (Just joking!)

Does he live nearby? That might be a good opportunity to ride your bike when it's not too cold, and if you spot him, start talking and fire up a con-

WEBwatch

IF YOU WERE A GARDEN

What kind of garden would you be? Fun on a lazy summer day. Don't work in the garden. BE a garden!
http://www.ivillage.com/home/garden/personality/quiz/

versation. What are the activities he is into away from school? Maybe you can manage to run into him and tell him that your relatives are taking forever to get this group "date" going, so why doesn't he do something with you?

Remember, the boy of your dreams might be the boy of your nightmares! But if you see both sides of his personality and really like him, and it seems as if he likes you, why don't you try asking him if he'd like to go out with you just as friends. You can't really hurry things along unless you make the first move.

GIFT IDEA! SUNDAE SURPRISE!

Sneak into your friend's house with the following: sundae fixings (ice cream, fudge and butterscotch toppings, whipped cream, chopped nuts, cherries, the works!). Don't forget dishes and spoons. Set everything up in the kitchen, and then call your friend in. It's a great surprise!

—Submitted by Nicole, 13

—Tiffany, 11, Canada

What If You're Crushing, but You're Too Shy to Do Anything About It?

The Problem Dear BoyZone: You have a crush, but you are way too shy to go up to the boy and ask him out. Would you write the question down on paper and put it in his locker or get a friend to ask him out for you?

—Trey, 11

What's the Hurry?

Everything takes time! Some things just need to go slowly; others go much faster. Take something you usually do, like making a sandwich or getting dressed, and time it to the second. Find out how long it takes you to do it. Then the next time, do it in half that time. Maybe you missed a sock or forgot to put away the mustard? Life is like that. When you hurry, you miss out on some important elements. Write about a time you hurried too much. What happened?

A Solution

Hey Trey! This seems wild, but it worked for me. The way I like to do it is come up with a way that he won't know who you are exactly. Do something like secretly put a note in his locker that asks him to play a game. At a certain time, when everyone is in the halls, he is to write down the names of all the girls he would go out with who pass his locker and don't look his way (of course, you'll be one of them walking by). Then he's to put the list in a certain place. You arrange for a guy or girl buddy to pick it up. Then you see if your name is on it! If it isn't, then you'll know and you won't have to be humiliated in front of people. Then the next day, if your name was on the list, tell him who you are and go from there. Or the more boring solution is you could just ask a friend if he's interested in you.

—Chastidy, 11, Georgia

There are times I look above and beyond There are times I feel your love around me I'll never forget When I feel that I don't belong Draw my strength From the words you said.
—From a Janet Jackson song "Together Again" Submitted by Amanda, 17, Colorado

I Attract Jerks and Repel Hotties!

The Problem

Dear BoyZone: Hi! OK, whenever I like this cute guy, he only likes me as a friend, and the guys I don't like

Q. I like a boy, but he does not like me. I am trying to get over him, but I can't. It is because every time I see him, I daydream about him. What would you do if this were happening to you?

—Noelle, 11, USA

1 I'd start looking around at school. Some other guy may be interested in me.

Mostly disagree   Somewhat disagree   Somewhat agree   Mostly agree

2 I'd make absolutely sure he didn't like me by asking his friends or just asking him out myself.

Mostly disagree   Somewhat disagree   Somewhat agree   Mostly agree

3 I'd get really interested in a project that would occupy my mind for a while, like a play, sport, school project (one that he won't be involved in, of course).

Mostly disagree   Somewhat disagree   Somewhat agree   Mostly agree

4 I'd write down exactly why I was so attracted to him and look for those qualities in another guy.

Mostly disagree   Somewhat disagree   Somewhat agree   Mostly agree

5 I'd ask my girlfriends to help me find another guy.

Mostly disagree   Somewhat disagree   Somewhat agree   Mostly agree

6 I'd ask his friends who he IS interested in and why he likes her.

Mostly disagree   Somewhat disagree   Somewhat agree   Mostly agree

or the guys I only like as friends like me. Is there something wrong with me? What can I do to stop attracting jerks and stop repelling hotties?

—Beth, 15

A Solution

Hey Beth! Beth, there is nothing wrong with you. There are always going to be times when you feel like you're never going to find a guy you like and who likes you back. But they will come along. You have to keep your eyes open. Also, remember that a friendship is a great foundation for a healthy boyfriend/girlfriend relationship because you know each other so well. So if you really like a guy, and he just wants to be friends, be friends. He might eventually discover that he does like you.

And it works the other way around; the guy you just want to stay friends with

TAKE THE COLOR QUIZ TOGETHER

Feel blue, red, and green today? What does that mean? Find out more about who you are and how you feel by taking the ColorQuiz. This site offers a free five-minute test that gives you colors to choose, then tells you something about yourself.

http://www.colorquiz.com/

EVER WONDER WHAT YOUR LIFE WOULD BE LIKE AS A GORILLA?

Are you most like Kuchi, the social butterfly? Or are you more like Taz, king of the pack? Take this quiz and find out you and your friend's gorilla personality profile. You'll never look at each other the same way again.

http://www.discovery.com /area/nature/gorillas/gorillas .html

you might eventually end up liking. So get to know him really well, talk to him, find out what he likes and dislikes. And make sure he gets the right impression about you. The most important thing to remember is to be yourself and you'll find the right guy.

—Lara, 14, Australia

Paint a Portrait

You don't have to use paint or markers; you can cut pictures from magazine or just use words. Create a portrait of your perfect guy. (This can't be anyone you know or any movie star or celeb. It must be a completely imaginary person.) Think about what qualities you want him to have or what color his hair might be. Do you want someone who is like you or not like you at all? There are billions of boys out there. If you know what you want, your odds of finding it go up right away!

Q. There is a very cute guy living on my street, but he is 13, in a higher grade, and he likes someone else. What would you do if this was happening to you?

—Sad Girl, 12, South Africa

1 I'd find out from his friends if he's serious about this other girl or is he really available.

Mostly disagree   Somewhat disagree   Somewhat agree   Mostly agree

2 I'd ask my parents to invite him and his parents over for a neighborhood party or dinner.

Mostly disagree   Somewhat disagree   Somewhat agree   Mostly agree

3 I'd have a party and invite him. Then I'd see for myself if he brings this other girl or not. If not . . . I'd go for him.

Mostly disagree   Somewhat disagree   Somewhat agree   Mostly agree

4 I'd take the direct approach. I'd ask him to be my date to the next school activity or dance. Hey, it's worth a try!

Mostly disagree   Somewhat disagree   Somewhat agree   Mostly agree

5 I'd find out where he hangs out after school, be there, and be friendly.

Mostly disagree   Somewhat disagree   Somewhat agree   Mostly agree

When Friends
Become Boyfriends

Can't a Guy Just Be a Friend?!

The Problem Dear BoyZone: There's a guy I like, just not "that way." If I'm friends with him, will he think I want to go out with him? If I have a guy for a friend, do you think that would make my boyfriend jealous? Do you think it's weird talking to a guy like I talk to my girl pals? Help!

—Confused in Canada,14

A Solution Dear Confused: Having a guy pal can make you feel more comfortable when you're around boys. A guy pal can help you understand how boys "tick." It can be hard to be friends with an ex-boyfriend but easy to befriend a guy you have never felt "romantic" about. He can tell you about his problems with girls, and you can help him understand. You can talk to him about your boyfriend. Sometimes you feel safer walking with a guy or taking a guy friend to a spur-of-the-moment party. If your boyfriend gets jealous, just explain that this guy is a pal, nothing romantic. Invite your boyfriend, your pal, and others out together so that your boyfriend can see you together and realize it's a friendship thing only. Understand that your boyfriend may have a girl pal that he doesn't feel romantic about. It's a two-way street.

Some Solutions

Realize that you may be good pals for life and attend each other's weddings. But things may change. He may start feeling attracted to you or you to him. Some of the best romances start out as "platonic" friendships. But if he develops a crush on you that you don't want, drop hints about a boy you wish would ask you out or remind him about your boyfriend. If this doesn't work, then be honest. You value this person so much as a pal, you can't ruin those feelings by risking a romance. His crush on you may pass naturally.

If you are the one who starts feeling romantic, drop hints about how everyone seems to think of you as a couple. Tell him how you've realized you like to spend time with him more than any other boy. Watch his body language or listen to how he reacts. OR you can just tell him how you feel. It might be hard if he doesn't feel the same way, but you might be able to get past this and keep your friendship. No matter which method you choose, choose SOMETHING. Just wishing he knew how you felt and looking "mooney-eyed" at him will just make him uncomfortable.

Good Luck!

—The BoyZone Columnists

Friend or Boyfriend? Where Are We Going?

The Problem Dear BoyZone: In the past two years, I have become very close to one of my guy friends. We are best friends, but sometimes it gets pretty intense. Sometimes I think he should be more of a boyfriend than my best friend, but I don't think things would be the same if he became my boyfriend. What should I do?

—Sidney, 14

A Solution   Hey Sidney! Most likely it won't be the same if you become his girlfriend. If your new relationship with him doesn't work out, do you want to risk losing one of your best friends? If you think your feelings are too strong, then let him know how you feel. Tell him you want to get involved; but if he doesn't want to, tell him that will be fine too.

One thing you want to look out for is if he says he doesn't want to get involved with you, then respect his wishes. When you are around him, don't make the situation weird for you or him by flirting and trying to get a romance started. Act friendly and natural. As bad as it may seem for you, it will make him feel more comfortable.

—Chastidy, 11, Georgia

He's on the Rebound. Do I Tell Him I Like Him?

The Problem   Dear BoyZone: I am having a problem. There is this boy about four houses up the street from me. I really like him and I think he likes me too. I want to tell him how I feel, but I am scared. I did it one time when we were walking

Q. Boys like me but just as a friend. They tell me all their troubles with other girls. I want a boyfriend. What would you do if this happened to you?

1 I'd tell them that I can't solve their problems and I'm not "Dear Abby." Grow up!

Mostly disagree   Somewhat disagree   Somewhat agree   Mostly agree

2 I'd listen and try to help but ask them if they have any friends who might want to go out with me.

Mostly disagree   Somewhat disagree   Somewhat agree   Mostly agree

3 I'd start flirting with them and change the subject . . . to me.

Mostly disagree   Somewhat disagree   Somewhat agree   Mostly agree

4 I'd join some new clubs or activities and meet some new boyfriend material.

Mostly disagree   Somewhat disagree   Somewhat agree   Mostly agree

5 I'd just listen and be friendly. Some day the right boy will just come along.

Mostly disagree   Somewhat disagree   Somewhat agree   Mostly agree

together, but he told me that he had a girlfriend. They broke up yesterday. What should I do? I think she is still after him and she doesn't like me.

—Kira, 12, Georgia

A Solution   Hey Kira! Well, that is a real problem. You like a boy who just broke up with his girlfriend, she still likes him, and she doesn't like you, AND you don't know how your crush feels. Well, what I think you should do is give him some time. Of course! He just finished with her, he may not know if he still likes her or not, and you don't want to make him feel even more confused, do you? So wait, and then . . . what?

Well, if he starts going out with her again, forget about it and get over him. But if he doesn't, tell him how you feel. Just tell him. If you are worried because you think that he may reject you, try to send some signals and see if he picks up on them. So what if his ex doesn't like you. If she's not a good friend of yours and he wants to be with you, so be it. I hope I helped you. Good luck! And remember, it is OK to ask for advice when you don't know what to do, but you should always do what YOU think is OK, and don't only think with your head, do it also with your heart.

—Irina, 12, Argentina

A CLASSIC IDEA FOR A CLASSY GUY

Does your dad or boyfriend like classic cars? Our town has a classic car rental. Bear Cats, Bentleys, 64 Mustangs, 59 Corvettes, 57 Thunderbirds, 63 Chevy Impalas. Save up your money and send your classic guy for a spin. Rent a driver if he doesn't have a license. Have a camera ready to take pictures.

—Submitted by Elisabeth, 17

Finding Yourself

Do you describe yourself as a "tomboy"? Or a "recluse"? Maybe this is how you were when you were younger, and now you'd like to experiment with some changes. Use this space to write down six things you'd want to try to feel more feminine. Examples: wear your hair up, paint your nails, wear a dress instead of pants. Every morning, pick one and try it out! If you're shy, write down six things you'd want to try to be more outgoing. Like take a dance class, learn an instrument, join a club.

1.	2.
3.	4.
5.	6.

Q. I have a guy friend who taught me how to dance the latest dances. I had no idea, but he expected to go to the prom with me. I already have a date. I don't want to hurt him. What would you do if this were happening to you?

—Sela, 16, Hawaii

1 I'd tell him how I feel. I like him, but as a friend. Nothing more. He'll get over it.

Mostly disagree   Somewhat disagree   Somewhat agree   Mostly agree

2 I'd find a girlfriend who likes him and tell her to ask him to the prom.

Mostly disagree   Somewhat disagree   Somewhat agree   Mostly agree

3 I'd have to think about it. Did I really say something that made him think I was going to go with him? If I did, I should go with him.

Mostly disagree   Somewhat disagree   Somewhat agree   Mostly agree

4 I'd tell him he's a great dancer and I really appreciate what he did for me, but I'd remind him that I never said I was going with him. Then I'd pick another big dance and tell him I'd go to that one.

Mostly disagree   Somewhat disagree   Somewhat agree   Mostly agree

5 I'd go out with both guys. Hey, lots of teens go in groups to the prom. We could be a trio.

Mostly disagree   Somewhat disagree   Somewhat agree   Mostly agree

Lifetime Friends, Until He Hit on Me!

The Problem   Dear BoyZone: One of my best friends that I grew up with started hitting on me on the couch when we were alone at his house watching a movie. I told him we should always stay just friends, and I think he took the hint. But now I don't talk to him as much because that incident totally makes me feel uncomfortable around him. What should I do?

—"Anonymous," 13, California

A Solution   Hey Anonymous! You should go up to him and ask him on your own if things have changed between you and say the reason why you didn't want to start a relationship was because you didn't want to risk losing your best friend if something went wrong. Don't just ignore him. It's like you are punishing him. Say that you want to stay friends, but at the end of the day if he's going to be stubborn, then there's nothing you can do about it. He may have too much of a crush on you so that hanging with you as friends now hurts him too much. Just wait for him to come to his senses and see what a great friend he'd be losing! Also, have you considered that you may be feeling "uncomfortable" because you DO have "boyfriend" feelings for him? Think about it.

—Zara, 12, England

My "Friend" Is Calling Me "Babe." Whazzup?

The Problem   Dear BoyZone: There is a guy in my class that I have known all my life and we are friends. Only recently, since we were made to sit next to each other, he has begun to act weird. He calls me "babe" and stuff, and I don't know if he is just goofing. HELP!! What should I do?

—Louise, 11

A Solution Hey Louise! My best bet is that he may like you. At your age boys, when they like a girl, act like two-year-olds. They can't just come out and say that they like you. I guess that it is just in their nature. If you don't think that this is what might be up, and since you said that you have been friends with this boy for a long time, just ask him straight up what is the problem. Maybe having you sit closer to him has made him suddenly realize that he likes you. If you think you might like him as b.f. material, ask him to a party or something. If you just want to stay friends and don't like him calling you "babe," then just tell him to stop it. If he is your friend, he will be grateful that you are being honest with him. I hope that this helps you.

MY FIRST PROM

Fill in the blanks and create a night you'll never forget.

http://www.agirlsworld.com /rachel/magic-story /myfirpro-val.html

TOGETHER

Explore the "Final Frontier" together. Not *Star Trek*! The International Space Station!

Take a virtual tour and watch a video of the station being assembled!

http://school.discovery.com /schooladventures/spacestation/

—Jen, 14, Washington

Q. I have a best friend and he is a guy, but I'm afraid if I tell my friends they will think I'm weird. This guy and I just enjoy going out together as friends. What would you do if this happened to you?

— Emma, 14, Australia

1   I'd tell my friends. They'll learn by the way we behave together that we truly are just friends.

    Mostly disagree   Somewhat disagree   Somewhat agree   Mostly agree

2 I'd say, who cares what our friends think? I'd just pal around with this guy as usual.

    Mostly disagree   Somewhat disagree   Somewhat agree   Mostly agree

3 I think it would be "weird" if my girlfriends expected me to go out with every guy I hung out with, and I'd tell them so.

    Mostly disagree   Somewhat disagree   Somewhat agree   Mostly agree

4 I'd tell my friends that this guy is my bud and they have to accept it.

    Mostly disagree   Somewhat disagree   Somewhat agree   Mostly agree

5 I'd have my buddy ask one of my gal pals out on a date. That would show them!

    Mostly disagree   Somewhat disagree   Somewhat agree   Mostly agree

Q. Up until a couple of weeks ago I was good mates with a boy from school, but in a game of "Truth or Dare" he revealed he had a crush on me. Now he goes all funny around me. How can I get our friendship back to normal? He barely even speaks to me anymore! What would you do if it happened to you?

—Jessica, 12, Scotland

1 I'd just be a pal and make a study date. I'd let him know that I miss the friendship.

Mostly disagree   Somewhat disagree   Somewhat agree   Mostly agree

2 If he "liked" me, I imagine that it may be too hard for him to be around me if he's really shy. I'd just be kind and let it go until he got up his courage again.

Mostly disagree   Somewhat disagree   Somewhat agree   Mostly agree

3 I'd really examine my own heart. Do I maybe have "boyfriend" feelings for him after all? If so, I'd tell him.

Mostly disagree   Somewhat disagree   Somewhat agree   Mostly agree

4 I'd just get a group activity together that includes some of his male pals and ask him to come. This may be easier for him.

Mostly disagree   Somewhat disagree   Somewhat agree   Mostly agree

5 I'd ask his friends to tell him that I still care, just not "that" way.

Mostly disagree   Somewhat disagree   Somewhat agree   Mostly agree

My Friends Laugh at My Best Guy Bud!

Dear BoyZone: I have this male friend, and he's got his first girlfriend, so he acts kind of weird. My other friends make fun of him a lot, and they talk about him behind his back. It really makes me mad! What should I do about it?

—Kelsey, 12

If you love somebody, let them go. If they come back, they are yours to love. If they don't, they never were.

—Anonymous
Submitted by
Valerie, 13, Pennsylvania

A Solution
Hey Kelsey! Hey, if they're real friends, they shouldn't be talking about him behind his back in the first place! He's just gotten a girlfriend, and in our stage of life we tend to act differently and see the world differently around us, but friends should be there to support us. You should tell off your so-called friends and say, "You may be my friends, but that doesn't give you the right to make fun of him. Wait until you fall in love!" :o)

Tell your male friend that they're making fun of him. He needs to know. And if you think he acts weird now that he has a girlfriend, tell him he should just be himself or else that girl is liking him for something he's not!

—Tiffany, 11, Canada

Stand Out in the Crowd

Everyone needs friends. It's great to have a group to hang out with, talk to, compare notes, and make plans. But don't get washed away in the tide. Just because "everyone" wears their hair long or eats hamburgers for lunch (or refuses to ever eat hamburgers at all!), decide how you feel about it. Write down what you really feel strongly about here. What issues do you take a stand on? No to drugs? Yes to honesty, even with your parents? No to dating wolves? No to pressure to do things you don't want? When all your friends say or do something that you disagree with, disagree out loud. You have the right and the responsibility to be an individual, even when it's hard. Of course, you can agree with your friends about anything, but you can't agree with anyone about EVERYTHING. Think for yourself.

When He Plays Hard to Get

The Problem Dear BoyZone: I have this one really good buddy who sees me as that: his buddy. But OH DEAR! He's SO cute. And I'm not the only one who thinks that. Just the other day in chorus he had girls surrounding him, but I was too nervous to go over there to them, so I hung back. Later when I went to talk to him, he asked me why I didn't come over. I really like him, but he's such a player! I don't know what to do. I heard from a friend that he likes me, too, but I'm afraid that he'd use me!

—Sign me Confused

A Solution Dear Confused: What your guy is doing is very normal. You said your friends told you that he likes you, and by the way he is acting it is probably true.

The reason he is surrounding himself with attention from those girls is probably because he wants you to see how appealing he is and how much he is liked by girls. You could say he is even trying to make you a little jealous.

CAN YOUR RELATIONSHIP WEATHER LOVE STORMS?

When the going gets tough, will your relationship last for the long haul?

http://homearts.com/depts /relat/67hwdyf1.htm

Some Solutions

If he ever comes up to you and asks, "Why didn't you come over?" you could say, "I am not into that kind of thing. I like talking to you better when we are alone."

If he is smart, then he will get exactly what you are trying to tell him. See, guys are very sensitive (believe it or not!). They send out little signals to see if you respond. In most cases, if you do respond, they will go further and maybe even ask you out.

When you didn't come over that time, he could have been a little mixed up. If you guys are buddies, and he really doesn't get that you want to be more than that, then you could drop hints yourself. Say, "I really like spending time with you." Eventually he will get your message and it is smooth sailing from then on.

Good luck!

—Lana K., 13, Indiana

Crushes

I'm Crushin' on a TV Star!

The Problem Dear Boy-Zone: I have this secret sort-of-crush on this guy on a TV show. His name is Jared. He's cute, funny, smart, and likes a lot of the same things I do. I'm scared to write a letter to him telling him how I feel because he probably gets a lot of those letters and will just be disgusted about mine. I don't know whether to go with my heart and write him or go with my other side that says I'll be utterly embarrassed. Please help!

—Cara, 13

*You're here, there's nothing I fear
And I know that my heart will go on.
We'll stay, forever this way
You are safe in my heart
And my heart will go on and on.*
—From "Love Theme" from *The Titanic* Submitted by Nancy, 11, North Dakota

Fan Mail

We all enjoy celebrities—that's why they're famous! Take some time and write a fan letter to someone you admire. It can be a TV star, a singer, an author, or maybe an athlete. Say why you admire him and maybe even how he inspires you to want to do the same kind of great things. Find an address for the person (it might be the TV station or record company) and mail it off! Real compliments are always enjoyed. And who knows—maybe you'll get a letter back! (I once wrote to an author I admired and was surprised and delighted that he answered me. We didn't become best friends, but it was fun.)

A Solution

Hey Cara! Hi! If you have a crush on the character this guy plays, then get over it, because that's not how the actor really is. That's not his personality. But if Jared is the actor and you like him, the real person, then you should write him a letter. Go for it!

Lots of actors love to get fan mail and try to answer it personally. However, when you write, do it just for fun. Don't expect to get a real-life, personal relationship started with this guy or you'll be hurt and disappointed.

ASK THE LOVE BUG!!

She'll help you with all your relationship problems! Start by asking Lovebug a "yes or no" question. After you ask the question, click the bar and get a girl-powered response.

http://www.agirlsworld.com /amy/pajama/valentines /lovebug.html

Here are some tips if you are afraid he won't answer or he won't like your letter. Include a photo of yourself. He will probably want to answer when he sees your cute face! Include a self-addressed stamped envelope so it will be easier for him to write back. Don't write a loooong letter; keep it short or else he won't even read it. Good luck!

—Irina, 13, Argentina

I'm Crushin' on My Male Friend's Relative!

The Problem

Dear BoyZone: This guy, I really like him. And I mean REALLY. He is related to one of my best male

Q. I'm friends with a boy at school and I'm crushin' on his best friend. I keep asking my friend to find out if my crush likes me but he says he "can't." What would you do if this happened to you?

—Anonymous, USA

1 I'd give up and ask another friend to find out.

Mostly disagree   Somewhat disagree   Somewhat agree   Mostly agree

2 I'd ask my friend why he won't help.

Mostly disagree   Somewhat disagree   Somewhat agree   Mostly agree

3 I'd just ask my crush to go out with me.

Mostly disagree   Somewhat disagree   Somewhat agree   Mostly agree

4 I'd ask my friend if he won't help because he likes me. (Hey, he might be jealous!)

Mostly disagree   Somewhat disagree   Somewhat agree   Mostly agree

5 I'd let my crush know how I feel in a note and slip it in his pocket.

Mostly disagree   Somewhat disagree   Somewhat agree   Mostly agree

friends (not a boyfriend) and I'm afraid that if I go with him, it will ruin me and my friend's friendship. What should I do?

—Caitlin, 13, USA

A Solution Hey Caitlin! If you really like this guy so much, then I think that first you should talk to your guy friend about it. Ask him if he would be okay if you went out with this guy you like. If this guy friend likes you just as a friend, there shouldn't be a problem. He could ask someone out and you could double date. But if he secretly likes you as a girlfriend, he might say that he would mind. And if he says he would mind, then you should talk to the guy you like and have him talk to your friend. (After all, they're related.) But I'm sure your friend will understand.

DISCOVER CUPID'S KITCHEN

Tasty gifts to make and yummy treats for sleepovers and parties.

http://www.agirlsworld.com /amy/pajama/valentines /val-kitchen.html

—Melissa, 12, Massachusetts

I'm Crushin' on an Older Guy.

The Problem Dear BoyZone: Help! I like a boy who's 15, but he doesn't know I exist! The worst part is, the other day when I went for a tennis tournament, I saw him there too. And he was talking to another girl, who's about my age. They were smiling and laughing and talking to each other. Don't laugh at me, but I'm afraid the girl is his girlfriend. I couldn't sleep the whole night thinking about him and that girl. What will I do?

—"E," 13

A Solution

Hey "E"! I know exactly how you feel. I'm sure you are an extremely cool gal. First, ask yourself a question. Is this a crush or real love? Two years difference in age is quite a lot. However, there might be a chance that he likes you. Why don't you go up to him and just be yourself? Get to know him better. Listen to what he likes, whether he's nice or inconsiderate, etc. Maybe, once you get to know him, you wouldn't think he's so wonderful after all. But, if he's a nice guy and you still like him, tell him or ask him out. If he doesn't want to commit to you, at least you can put the crush behind you, right? And if he does like you, CONGRATULATIONS! Good luck!

—Dani, 14, Malaysia

WEB watch

BREAK THE ICE

Explore the world of dreams together.

What do your dreams mean? What's the best stage of sleep to whisper sweet nothings into your loved ones ears so they will remember?

http://library.thinkquest.org /C005545/

Q. What do you do if your crush is an over-achiever who wants to do nothing but study, even though he's an "A" student?

—Anonymous, USA

1 I'd study with him and suggest that I need to take a "fun" break (movie, game, snackfest, etc.).

Mostly disagree   Somewhat disagree   Somewhat agree   Mostly agree

2 I'd discover what he really likes to do when not studying and build a party around it.

Mostly disagree   Somewhat disagree   Somewhat agree   Mostly agree

3 I'd praise him for his great study habits and ask if he can help me learn how to study better (it's a way to spend quality time with him).

Mostly disagree   Somewhat disagree   Somewhat agree   Mostly agree

4 I'd dump him. He's a nerd. Go for more "fun" guys.

Mostly disagree   Somewhat disagree   Somewhat agree   Mostly agree

5 I'd quiz him on what he's learned (for a test) and convince him that he's ready. It's time to celebrate and party!

Mostly disagree   Somewhat disagree   Somewhat agree   Mostly agree

I'm Crushin' on My Best Friend's Older Bro!

The Problem Dear BoyZone: There is this hot guy in 7th grade, and he is 13. I am in 5th grade and 11. He is my best friend in the world's big brother! She hates him. She said it was sick to like your best friend's brother, but I totally disagree. She said he likes me. How can I tell my friend that I like her brother without embarrassing myself in front of her and her brother and his friends?

—Renee, 11

Your words are my food, your breath my wine. You are everything to me.

—Sarah Bernhardt
Submitted by
Rachel, 11, New Mexico

A Solution Hey Renee! In what way does your best friend's brother like you? Just in a sisterly way or in THAT way? He might just like you in a sisterly way. There's nothing "sick" about liking a friend's brother, but at 13 he's a teen; and I don't mean to pour cold water all over you, but guys at his age don't usually like much younger girls. The age gap is just too big somehow. When you're both in your teens, it doesn't matter so much. But if you really must, tell your best friend and get her to keep it to herself and get her to somehow ask her brother in a casual way. Then if he says yes, he does like you in that way, then good for you. Or you could just take the chance and get it all settled in one move. Ask him out! Maybe invite him to a party where there will be other kids his age as well. If he says he can't, then he probably just likes you as a sister. Anyway, good luck!

—Dani, 15, Malaysia

Consider the Path Before You

When you are romantically interested in someone, try this little game. Imagine that this page is a game board. Draw and color and decorate it with possibilities. What would he do if I invited him out? His reaction would be a) Run, b) Say Yes, c) Say Maybe Later, or d) Come to meet my family first. Plan out "If I say this, then his reaction could be" or "If I do this, the next thing to happen could be A, B, or C." As you know, it's never so simple as telling a guy you like him, and then he tells you that he likes you too. So consider the path you walk to be as filled with possibilities as grains of sand on a beach! (There is a mythological Greek hero named "Prometheus," and his name translates as "forethought." That's why he was a hero—he considered the results of his actions before he did something!) Have fun filling this page.

Q. Why do guys want you to ask your friend out for them? I feel funny about it. What would you do if this were happening to you?

—Asteroid-Female, 12, Washington

1 I'd realize that guys are sometimes shy. Then I'd go ahead and do it for him, as a friend.

Mostly disagree   Somewhat disagree   Somewhat agree   Mostly agree

2 First I'd talk to my friend and find out if she likes him. If yes, I'd go back to the guy and tell him whazzup. Then he can ask for himself.

Mostly disagree   Somewhat disagree   Somewhat agree   Mostly agree

3 I'd tell him the truth. I don't want to be a go-between.

Mostly disagree   Somewhat disagree   Somewhat agree   Mostly agree

4 I'd see if my friend likes him, and if she says yes, I'd tell her to ask him out. I'd explain that he's afraid of rejection.

Mostly disagree   Somewhat disagree   Somewhat agree   Mostly agree

5 I'd have a party, invite them both, and tell him to go for it.

Mostly disagree   Somewhat disagree   Somewhat agree   Mostly agree

I'm Going with a Guy, but My Three-Year Crush Asked Me Out!

The Problem Dear BoyZone: I've got a problem! For the past almost three years I have really liked this guy. I am shy, so I never wanted to talk to him. We wave to each other and say hi and things, but nothing big. About a month ago . . . HE ASKED ME OUT! I never thought that this would ever happen, but I had to say no because over the past year, I've had a boyfriend. I love my boyfriend, and I don't want to end it. Should I be friends with this other guy or what? HELP!!!

—Bryn, 17

A Solution Hey Bryn! I think that you should tell your boyfriend of a year that you want to try seeing other people for a while and that if you both don't like it, then you will see each other only and that is it. Then you can ask your three-year crush out and see what happens. Maybe you two were meant to be; you just have to find out first. If you don't find out, you'll always wonder. But one more thing . . .

TOGETHER: LEARN THE SECRET LANGUAGE OF FLOWERS

Give a Moss Rosebud to say love has started and a white and red rose together for unity. Discover flowers, the secret language of romance.

http://www.dina.kvl.dk/~fischer /alt.romance/flowers.html

if you do go out with this other guy, everything will seem great at first—all relationships do, especially since you've been in the same relationship for a whole year and something new is exciting. So just don't go too fast; and remember, everything changes, and then it changes again. You're still young.

—Rachael, 17, Florida

He's Pretending to Crush on My Cousin!

GIFT IDEA: KIDNAPPED!

Call your boyfriend's mom and all your friends. Set up a "kidnap" breakfast. You sneak into your boyfriend's house and kidnap him in his pajamas! Do it real early in the morning and take him to Denny's.

—Submitted by Charlene, 12

The Problem Dear Boy-Zone: There is a guy in my kickboxing club. I'm afraid to ask him out 'cuz it might hurt my cousin's feelings 'cuz he is pretending to go out with her. I know he likes me 'cuz he told me. The only problem is we are very close friends, and a relationship could very well end, and it might end our friendship as well. And what about my cousin?

—Adrieanne, 13, Ireland

A Solution Hey Adrieanne! Is this guy really worth it if he's only "pretending" to go out with your cousin? If he's just trying not to hurt her feelings, you should tell him you can't go out with him unless he's honest with your cousin. If he's just being cruel, however, he's not worth it as a friend or a boyfriend.

If you decide to go out with him, your cousin will be angry, no doubt, but she'll probably realize that friends are more important than boys. It can be dangerous to go out with someone you're already close to, so before you go out with this boy, you should check that you actually like him and are not just going out with him because he likes you. Don't go out with him if the relationship is unlikely to last because it could be a tragic waste of a friendship.

—Lauren, 14, Scotland

I've Got a Crush on a "Wolf." Now What?

The Problem Dear Boy-Zone: I started a new school this year, and I am a freshman. I met a senior, and I really like him. But I am not sure if I want to go out with him. I have heard from some people that he likes me too and wants to get to know me better. But from others I have heard that he just wants to use me. I know that he is older and obviously has experience that I don't. My friend also likes him; he supposedly liked her last year. They are still friends.

—Scared, 15

WHAT'S YOUR FITNESS PERSONALITY?

Are you and your beloved compatible? What if you're a Racer and he's a Stroller? Or maybe you're both Dancers and Trekkers. Knowing which type you are means you know what kind of fun to have together. Take the quiz and see for yourself. You'll find it at this site.

http://www.accenthealth
.com/hl/cooltools/1999
/personality/personality.html

A Solution Dear Scared: Boy, reading your problem brought back memories! Being a freshman is hard enough without worrying about stuff like guys, right? But back to your problem. You're being really smart about the whole situation, thinking before you get into it, because sad as it is, there are a lot of guys who have that macho, ego thing going where they just want to mess around with as many girls as they can so they can be "cool." And, unfortunately, a lot of times that's what senior guys want from freshman girls.

At my school, the senior guys actually have a contest for the first three months of school to see how many "fish girls" they can bag (how mature is that?), and it's really hard because this guy is probably so cute and so sweet (and did I mention cute?). Going out with an older guy makes you feel really cool. I mean, you're walking down the halls, and all the other girls stare, and he drives you to school, and it's just perfect. But most of the time you won't actually be going out with him, just messing with him when he wants you to.

And you're right, he probably does have a lot more experience than you, and he'll expect a lot more from you. So really it's kind of like the luck of the draw; you just have to hope that your Prince Charming isn't a pig. But anyway, here are my solutions. Analyze the situation: How long has he "wanted to get to know you better"? If it's been awhile, say a month or so, he probably is genuinely interested, but don't go jumping into his arms yet . . . how far into the school year is it? Judging from my experience, the longer the better, meaning that if school started in September and it's February, that's a good sign.

How many girls has he already hooked up with this year? If he's even been rumored to have messed around with more than

> ## " You Can Quote Me on That "
>
> *Don't say you love me,*
> *Don't say you need me,*
> *I really don't think*
> *that's fair.*
> *Boy, I'm not so dumb,*
> *But when you leave me*
> *I'll be wishing I,*
> *wishing I,*
> *wishing I was there*
> *with you.*
>
> From Natalie Imbruglia's song
> "Wishing I Was There"
> Submitted by
> Meghan, 12, USA

one girl a month, he's probably not exactly into you for your brains, so I advise major caution if you do decide to pursue this boy.

Have you ever actually talked to him? This question is important in any crush, regardless of the beau's age and/or reputation. If all's well, I say go for it! Use your mutual friend to drop hints, smile at him, whatever it is you do to get a man. But you said your friend is into him too? Well, babe, hate to break it to you, but that's another problem, and I probably shouldn't waste more of your time trying to solve that one. So just remember, a wise woman once said, "Never drop a girlfriend for a boyfriend!" Best of luck!

—Sara, 14

My Best Friend Is the Link to My Crush. How Can I Stop Using Her?

The Problem Dear BoyZone: My best friend has a next-door neighbor who is SO CUTE! When I first met him, we hit it off great. I went everywhere with her just so I could be with him. Now I feel guilty, like I'm using her to get to him. Her birthday party came up, and he was there. We talked the whole time—for 8 hours. But now I think she's suspicious. But how can I let him know that I TRULY like him? I'm going crazy! I call my friend trying to think of ways to go over to her house without sounding weird. What can I do to get to him and not use my friend?

—Tiffany, 12

TOGETHER TO THE JIGZONE

Do an online jigsaw puzzle together. It can be as easy as 6 pieces or as hard as 247.

http://www.jigzone.com/

A Solution   Hey Tiffany! You should never let a boy get in the way of friendship. Boys will come and go, and you are only 12 years old. So that means there will be so many more guys in your life than this one. Don't chase after this one. No guy is worth chasing after. If you do chase them, they will not truly like you. Plus, there might be something about this guy that you do not know about, and you might not like it. I think you should tell your friend up front what you have been doing. Real friends should never have secrets kept from one another. Here is a story that happened to me.

One of my friends is a guy. Over the summer I went to his house to swim in his pool. His best friend, who is his neighbor, was over there too. We sort of hit it off, but after I left my friend's house, I realized that his neighbor wasn't the kind of guy that I wanted. He was rude, said a lot of bad things, and he acted like a hot shot. Make sure you know more about him before you zero in on him.

Now, if you really need to hook up with this guy, get his phone number. If you don't want to ask your friend for his number, then

They were two souls with but a single thought, two hearts that beat as one.

—John Keats
Submitted by
Samantha, 13, United Kingdom

ask him directly or ask a guy friend of his next time you get to-gether. Here is just a little advice for you. Please don't call your friend all the time trying to go over to her house just to see the guy you like. It is not polite to use someone that way. I hope everything turns out the way you want it to!

—Casey, 14, Tennessee

Family, Friends, and Boyfriends

The Guy I Like Is My Parents' Worst Nightmare!

The Problem Dear BoyZone: There is this boy that I like but my family doesn't like him because he steals and curses. What should I do?

— Melanie, 11

A Solution Hey Melanie! I have to tell you, this is a difficult situation. You are in a period of your life where what you want and like is not always what your parents want and like (for example, you disagree because they don't think the boy you like is OK for you). Differences and fights between you and your parents are totally normal. That shows that you are growing up and trying to find your own identity. Let's go back to your problem. Your parents cannot decide who you like, but they can decide who you go out with. So, if you don't like the decision they make (they won't let you go out with the boy you like), you can try to convince them.

First, however, you have to ask yourself why you like the boy. If he steals and curses, do you want him in your life? If you "are together," what he does will reflect on you. If you realize you don't actually like him, the problem is over. But if you still like him, then you have to talk to your parents. Tell them how you feel, why you like the boy, why you think they should let you go out with him. If you tell them why you think they should, and they agree, the problem is over. If they still say no, you are going to have to get over it. You are only 11 years old. You have a lot of time to like boys and have relationships with them. Besides, like I said before, you and only you can decide who you like.

—Irina, 12, Argentina

His Family Doesn't Approve.

The Problem   Dear BoyZone: If a boy you really like is a pastor's son at a church and the pastor doesn't approve of it even though you're a good member of the church, what would you do?

—Tela, 12

A Solution   Hey Tela! The way I see it is that if the pastor, this boy's father, doesn't approve of you liking this boy, then chances are his mother and close relatives do not approve much of it either. If this is so, then I would not try to ask him out, or really flirt with him. Just be friendly.

If you sneak around behind his family, you'll get in trouble one way or another. His family could find out, or the boy could tell his parents. This does not mean that you cannot be good friends with him or should stop having feelings for him. But I would take caution when around his family. Be yourself, be friendly. Maybe he'll make the move and ask you out. Then, he'll have to deal with the disapproval, not you.

—Alex, 11, USA

WEBwatch

WHICH ANIMAL ARE YOU?

Lion? Tiger? or Bear? Oh, my!

Check out this site.

http://www.animals.sites.cc/

What Do You Do When Your First Date Includes His Little Brother?

The Problem Dear BoyZone: I met this really cool guy! He gave me a box of chocolates for Valentine's Day, but we weren't really close then. We had hardly met. I didn't get him anything. He asked me to go to the movies with him, and I was really excited until I found out his little brother was coming, and he is a pain! What should I do?

—Ashley, 14

A Solution Dear Ashley: You may just have to be a good sport about it and let the brother come. I have two brothers, and they are both a pain. But if I invited someone to the movies and they said they didn't really want to go, I would be hurt very badly. He might just be testing you. What if he thinks that if

When You Write the Rules

The world is full of parents, and parents are full of rules. Maybe your parents are easygoing, but your friends' parents are super strict. For now, you have to respect that there are limits on what you can do. But think about when you grow up (off to college or working at a career) and consider what rules you might like to keep. Not allowed to stay out all night? Maybe you're really happy to be home and asleep by midnight. Breaking the rules doesn't require any thought. Write down the rules you're going to set for your kids when you're a parent. Deciding which rules work for you is a good way to start on your independence.

you can put up with this monster, you can put up with anything? If you refuse to go, back out at the last minute, or get "sick," he will be really insulted. Just try to put up with it for one movie. How long will it be, 2 1/2 hours at the most? In a dark building! If the manager kicks you out, just go to McDonald's or someplace like that. That will show him that you can put up with his little brother. Who knows, the brother might not even be there with you! I think this is a test, and personally I wouldn't want to fail!

Good Luck!

—A BoyZone columnist

WEBwatch

THE 1900 HOUSE

What would it be like to live in 1900? Meet a modern family that stepped back into time, wearing the clothes, eating the food, and doing the chores of a 1900s family. Something fun to do while you're waiting for him to call.

http://www.pbs.org/wnet /1900house/

Not Allowed to Date. I'll Go Nutz!

The Problem Dear BoyZone: I was going out with this guy called Adam, and I was not allowed to go see movies and stuff with him cause my parents said I am too young and can only go out when I am 15. I was so upset and I bring up the issue almost every day. What should I do? Go out with him secretly? Live in misery till I am 15? Ignore my parents?

—Sophia, 12

Q. There is a guy at my school who I really like. We think that we are old enough to go on a date, but our parents don't think we are old enough. What would you do if this were happening to you?

— Darica, 13, Kansas

1 I'd go on a "supervised" date where one of our parents comes along. Hey, it's better than nothing.

Mostly disagree   Somewhat disagree   Somewhat agree   Mostly agree

2 I'd arrange to see him secretly.

Mostly disagree   Somewhat disagree   Somewhat agree   Mostly agree

3 I'd get both sets of parents together and convince them to let us have a "trial" date. If we both act responsibly, then they'll let us date.

Mostly disagree   Somewhat disagree   Somewhat agree   Mostly agree

4 I'd convince my parents to let us go on a "group" date with three or four other "couples" our age.

Mostly disagree   Somewhat disagree   Somewhat agree   Mostly agree

5 I'd just wait until I was older and just see each other at parties and at school. Maybe my parents are right. We aren't old enough. There's plenty of time.

Mostly disagree   Somewhat disagree   Somewhat agree   Mostly agree

— Edited by Margaret, 15, Arkansas

A Solution

Hey Sophia! Your parents don't let you go out because they're afraid you might get hurt. Talk to your parents in a really nice way. Make a compromise. Perhaps your parents will let you go out if you bring a few girlfriends along? Plan girl/boy parties with friends at the home of someone your parents trust. Maybe they would let you go out with a group of boys and girls. Meanwhile, spend time with Adam in school or at after-school activities. Eat lunch together; get assigned to school projects with him. You can both volunteer to work on a school fair or other charity project. Then you would see him, but it wouldn't be a "date" and would be supervised by adults so your parents should be happy. Hope it's all solved soon. Good luck!

—Dani, 15, Malaysia

HARRY POTTER PRONUNCIATION GUIDE

Tired of arguing with your sweetheart about how to pronounce Voldemort or Hermione? This Web site will help.

http://www.scholastic.com /harrypotter/books /pronunciation/play.htm

He's Older. Should I Date Him on the Sly?

The Problem

Dear BoyZone: I like this guy who's almost 18, and I'm 13. We are good friends but I don't know if he likes me. My mom says I can't date him. I think I know why. He

Journalize It!

Too Young for What?

Your parents have known you all of your life, and of course they care about you very much. There are some things that you really do need to be a certain age for. Imagine a 10-year-old behind the wheel of a car, or a 13-year-old running for governor. Although you are sure you are old enough, the truth is that your parents are going to make you wait. While you're waiting, why not get ready? Look at the adults around you who have romantic relationships, and study how it works. Write or draw what you see about their relationships that you like. Maybe they spend a lot of time talking, maybe they both like to jog in the morning, maybe they both work, or maybe they like to eat at home or go out to restaurants. See how falling in love can lead to being together—and know that you have years before you need to decide what kind of relationships you want to have.

sleeps with all his g/f's, but I wouldn't do that. Should I sneak and date him?

— Eva, 13, USA

A Solution

Hey Eva! If your mom doesn't want you to date a guy older than you, then you should listen to her. If your mom found out, she would be really upset and she might not trust you about guys anymore. You should just stay friends with him for now. (*Editor's note:* When you are older, five years isn't much of a difference. But there's a lot of difference between 13 and 18. I know you like him, but he's probably just your friend. Besides, you know he sleeps with his girlfriends, so take the hint. One wrong move and you could put this guy away for life. Underage is underage. And please don't put yourself in a bad situation and hurt your mom by dating him secretly.)

— Melissa, 12, Massachusetts

GET YOUR PERSONALITY SORTED HERE!

The Keirsey Temperament Sorter will ask you a million questions, but the outcome is usually very interesting! Find it at this Web site.

http://www.advisorteam.com /user/kts.asp

FABLES AND FUN FACTS: AMO, AMAS, AMAT!

Read these international customs and superstitions about Love.

http://www.agirlsworld.com /amy/pajama/valentines /storytime.html

The best proof of love is trust.

—Dr. Joyce Brothers
Submitted by
Kacy, 15, New York

Journalize It!

Admiring the Bad Boys? Maybe You're Looking for a Dare!

It can seem romantic or exciting to get involved with a boy who is "bad"—much older, sophisticated, running with a dangerous crowd. Maybe what you are really looking for is your own "shadow" side. A girl who makes her bed every morning and washes the dishes every night may dream about riding motorcycles or dancing in nightclubs. Maybe what you admire in HIM is something you'd like to see in YOU. Make a list of "dangerous" things you'd like to do—surfing, bungee jumping, karate, sailing, rock climbing. See if you could take a class, or have a parent or an older sibling go with you. Don't follow someone else to admire their qualities. Develop your own!

Q. My boyfriend and I have been going out for about three months now. But my mom won't let us go anywhere together. During school vacations, I don't see him at all. We only talk on the phone. What would you do if this were happening to you?

—Lauren, 12, Georgia

1 I'd try the group date thing. I'd get several couples together and tell my mom we're going with a bunch of kids and invite her to come supervise.

Mostly disagree   Somewhat disagree   Somewhat agree   Mostly agree

2 I'd talk to his parents first. If his parents think it's okay, then I'd ask his 'rents to talk to mine about it.

Mostly disagree   Somewhat disagree   Somewhat agree   Mostly agree

3 If my mom insisted that we couldn't be alone together, I'd invite her to go with us to a movie. The only thing is, she wouldn't get to sit with us. She'd have to sit a few rows behind or away from us. Hey, it's better than nothing.

Mostly disagree   Somewhat disagree   Somewhat agree   Mostly agree

4 I'd ask my boyfriend to have a party at his house. Maybe my mom would let me go to a supervised party.

Mostly disagree   Somewhat disagree   Somewhat agree   Mostly agree

5 If there's a school dance, I'd ask my mom to volunteer to be one of the chaperones. Then at least my boyfriend and I could go together.

Mostly disagree   Somewhat disagree   Somewhat agree   Mostly agree

I'm Not Allowed to Talk to Boys on the Phone! He Keeps Calling!

The Problem Dear BoyZone: There is this boy I like, but I am not allowed to talk to boys on the phone. He is always calling my house and I tell him he can't, but he doesn't listen. I like him, so what should I do?

—Sandy, 13

A Solution Hey Sandy! I think you should do two things here.

CHECK OUT THE SODA CONSTRUCTOR

Guys totally dig on this site (and girls do too!). It's a cool interface that lets you build your own creatures quickly and easily. Sure, they're just lines; but add mass (weight) and gravity, and they take on personalities. Watch the results.

http://sodaplay.com/index.htm

1. First, speak to your parents (if they are the ones not allowing you to speak to boys on the phone), and ask them why you're not being allowed. Tell them that these boys are your friends, just like the girls who call your house, and you would like to be able to talk to them without feeling that you are doing something wrong.

Tell them that although you understand and respect their concerns for you, you are 13 years old and should be allowed to speak to your friends, even if they are boys. After all, what harm can a telephone call do? If you are calm and understanding and approach them at a good time, they may well listen to what you have to say and even allow you to start talking to boys on the phone occasionally.

2. If your parents refuse to go into this and just continue to forbid you to talk to boys on the phone, you have no other choice but to speak to the boy instead. Ask him why he continues to call when he knows your parents forbid it, and ask him if he would stop for a while. Then you can discuss things with your parents and try to get them to see reason. Tell him that you like talking to him but just can't at the moment, and perhaps if he actually comes around to your house occasionally, your parents might be more likely to let you talk to him then. And if they see that he is actually harmless, they may allow the odd phone call too.

If it is all too embarrassing having him round at your house (which I well understand), then you will either have to get another adult to have a word with your parents (maybe an adult will be able to persuade them to let you speak to boys on the phone), or you will just have to see this boy at different times. You could arrange to meet him on the weekends, ask him to parties or other social events, and just wait for your mum to realize you're growing up. Eventually she'll have to start letting you talk to boys on the phone. So just be patient until then!

WEB watch

LEARN THE LANGUAGE OF LOVE

Love in days gone by . . . Language of Love offers a look at the customs of dating and romance during Victorian times. Jane Austin fans will love this site!

http://www.stormi.com/luv.html

—Shannon, 15, England

Journalize It!

Face Time

We all spend a lot of time on the phone, and online, chatting. Next time you hear from a friend, make a date to talk face to face. Notice how facial expression and gestures enhance the conversation. Consider the difference of communication between talking on the phone and talking in person. Then write down your thoughts.

My Best Friend Dumped Me to Hang with Guys!

The Problem Dear BoyZone: Hey, my friend chooses her male friends over me all the time now. I've been friends with her for almost three years, and she's only known one of her male friends, whom she chooses over me most of the time, for only a year. I'm trying not to be jealous, but it's hard when every time I call her she doesn't want to talk because she is talking to them! Please help!

— Dominique, 15

A Solution Hey Dominique! I can certainly understand how you feel, and it is hard to keep yourself from being jealous. Your friend probably chooses these guys over you because guys are new and exciting. Don't think of it as her choosing them over you, though. You will always be her best friend; those guys are just temporary. She won't be excited by them forever. Maybe if you try to understand her better, then she will include you. Try asking her questions about these guys and act all interested, and maybe she will want you to go

You Can Quote Me on That

Never thought I would find love so sweet,
Never thought I would meet someone like you.
Well now I've found you and I'll tell you no lie.
This love I've got for you Could take me 'round the world.
Now show me love.

—From a Robyn song, "Show Me Love" Submitted by Vanessa, 13, Oklahoma

Learn to Be Committed

One of the most important things in life is setting your priorities. When you make a commitment or a promise, remember that it's important to keep it. You wouldn't want other people breaking their promises to you! Take a simple matter and make a commitment or two right here. Think of it as an exercise, strengthen your "promise" muscle. You could promise to make your bed every day, and do it. Or help to make dinner one night a week, or finish your homework before you get online to chat. When you commit to a friendship, it's very similar. You have to decide where your friends fit into your life. Part of friendship is creating trust, and when you have trust and commitment, you have a solid foundation to build on. What commitments have you made to your friends? Write them here.

along with her and her new guy friends to the next place they go. Maybe her new guy friend will also have a friend who feels left out, and he will go too. Maybe you'll like him. You never know.

—Rachael, 17, Florida

THINK ME

I think . . . therefore I am. This ThinkQuest site is all about who YOU are, and your personality.

http://library.thinkquest.org /C004361/

My Friends Think He's Not Good Enough!

The Problem Dear Boy-Zone: What do you do if your friends don't think the guy you like is "good enough"? I really like this guy, but my friends say he's not good enough. I think he's just misunderstood. I really like him, but my friends keep criticizing him and saying that I'm too good for him.

What should I do? And my friends make fun of me because of the guys I like.

Sometimes the heart sees what is invisible to the eye.

—Jackson Brown
Submitted by
Tenielle, 12, Australia

Q. My stepdad and his son just moved in with us. My stepbrother is such a hottie! I'm attracted to him. After all, I'm not related to him. What would you do?

—Anonymous, USA

1 I'd tell my mom and hope she can figure out what to do.

Mostly disagree   Somewhat disagree   Somewhat agree   Mostly agree

2 I'd keep quiet and try to ignore him.

Mostly disagree   Somewhat disagree   Somewhat agree   Mostly agree

3 I'd just try to be a friend to him.

Mostly disagree   Somewhat disagree   Somewhat agree   Mostly agree

4 I'd talk to a counselor or nonfamily adult—fast. This is serious.

Mostly disagree   Somewhat disagree   Somewhat agree   Mostly agree

5 I'd let him know how I feel and work it out together.

Mostly disagree   Somewhat disagree   Somewhat agree   Mostly agree

They say they're stupid and stuff like that. Should I stop dating those guys or tell my friends that I like them and that's all that matters?

—Allison, 13, and Allison, 12

A Solution

Hey Allisons! Ask your friends why he's not "good enough." There might be something your friends know that you don't. And they just want the best for you. But the most likely explanation is that your friends just don't know him well or know him simply by reputation (a bad one, most likely). Arrange a time when your friends and your boyfriend can get together, talk to all of them and find out if they have anything in common. You want them to get to know the guy you like and know who he is.

If they still don't get along, just compromise. You can still be friends with them and keep your boyfriend. If you really like him, never let your friends stop you from going out with him.

FUNfest

A GIFT FOR YOUR SWEETIE!

You can make your own rock candy! It's fun, it's pretty, and it tastes great!

What you'll need: Sugar, water, pencil, jar, paperclip, string

How to make it: Boil 1 cup of sugar for 5 minutes, then let it cool. (Don't set the burner too high. It'll burn the sugar.) Empty boiled sugar in a jar. Tie a string to a pencil and put a paperclip at the other end of string. Put the pencil on the jar so the paperclip is in the boiled water. Let it sit for a couple of days and be patient, then your sugar rock candy will grow!

—Submitted by Ashlee, 12

Friends are like that sometimes; they feel jealous and worry that if you date your guy, they'll lose your friendship. It's okay for them to feel this way; it's growing up. You know them all best; you know inside you the right decision. But never dump your guy just because your friends don't like him, and vice-versa. Spend time with both of them.

—Lara, 14, Australia

What Do You Do When You and Your Best Friend Like the Same Guy?

Editor's Note: Here's another look at a familiar question.

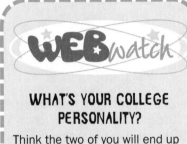

WHAT'S YOUR COLLEGE PERSONALITY?

Think the two of you will end up at a big school together? Or is a tiny arts college the place to build your dreams? Find your college personality at this site.

http://www.usnews.com /usnews/edu/college/cpq /coquiz.htm

The Problem Dear Boy-Zone: I am in big trouble. My best friend likes the same guy I do. Please help me!

—Marina, 11

A Solution Dear Marina: This happens a lot, and I know from experience that it can turn out bad. It can also turn out pretty good!

I think you should find out somehow, maybe through his friends or have one of your friends ask him, if he likes one of you. If he does, then whichever girl he likes should talk to the other girl about it. If it doesn't hurt her feelings too bad, maybe this boy and the lucky girl have a chance together.

If that does work out, the girl who didn't "get him" should find another boy who's nice and likes her. Then both of you would be happy. If it hurts one of your feelings, though, you should just forget about a relationship with him and you could both be friends with him.

It is not worth losing your friendship over a guy! Boyfriends are only temporary, but friendships are forever!

Good Luck!

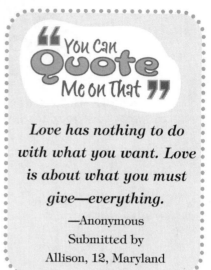

" You Can Quote Me on That "

Love has nothing to do with what you want. Love is about what you must give—everything.

—Anonymous
Submitted by
Allison, 12, Maryland

—Chelsea F., 12, Las Vegas, Nevada

I Think My Best Friend Lied About Me to My Crush!

The Problem   Dear BoyZone: I love one boy from my class since we got to this school, and he knows it. When I started to think that I'm finally doing the right things and he's starting to like me, suddenly he started to say bad things about me and go with my best friend a lot. I can't prove this, but I think my best friend told him total lies about me. Right now he doesn't talk

Q. Your older sister has a new boyfriend and he asked YOU out! What would you do?

—Anonymous, USA

1 I'd tell my sister, and if she didn't care, then I'd go out with him.

Mostly disagree   Somewhat disagree   Somewhat agree   Mostly agree

2 I'd tell him no way and never tell my sister he asked. She'd be too hurt.

Mostly disagree   Somewhat disagree   Somewhat agree   Mostly agree

3 I'd tell my sister that she should dump him because he isn't true to her.

Mostly disagree   Somewhat disagree   Somewhat agree   Mostly agree

4 I'd tell him no and say that if he doesn't tell my sister that he asked me out, I'll tell her myself.

Mostly disagree   Somewhat disagree   Somewhat agree   Mostly agree

5 I'd go out with him and hope she doesn't find out.

Mostly disagree   Somewhat disagree   Somewhat agree   Mostly agree

with me, and I haven't done anything bad. It's her doing. I can feel it in my bones. I really don't know what to do.

—Maitel, 12

A Solution Hey Maitel! I think the first thing you should do is confront your best friend. But before you do this, make sure you're right about her. Ask her what happened. Also, since she has been going out with him, she should know why he started saying bad things about you. But if she won't tell you, talk to the guy you like. Ask him why and explain yourself. Maybe it's because of something you did that you're not aware of. Just see what happens. If he doesn't believe you, then I think it's better if you just forget him. If your friend did "badmouth" you, you must work it out or drop her.

—Dani, 14, Malaysia

WEB*watch*

GREAT LOVE SONNETS

"Shall I Compare Thee to a Summers Day?" Looking for a romantic poem?

Check out this site. Spice up your locker notes.

http://albionmich.com /valentine.html

My Best Friend Blabbed to My Crush. Now He's Avoiding Me!

The Problem Dear BoyZone: I've had a MAJOR crush on this guy for about a year. Then one day, he asked me out! We

Importance of Honesty

Everyone lies. We've all done it. Telling your Mom that you brushed your teeth already, telling your friend that color is lovely on her when it makes her look like a ripe apple . . . Little lies can be a bad habit, even if we convince ourselves they are not that bad. Write down three lies you've told—big or little—and how you feel about having told them. Decide to go for one day and be honest about everything. (Maybe pick a day when you won't be at school, or when your usual honesty challenges aren't around.) The best part of being honest is that you don't have to remember what you said to everybody!

went out on our date and had a good time. The next day, I was telling my friends about it. Then one of my best female friends admits she has had a crush on him for a long time too!! Then she goes and tells my guy the whole situation (that we both like him)! He gets all freaked out, and now he's avoiding both of us!!! What should I do?

— Nikki, 13, New Mexico

A Solution   Hey Nikki! The classic sticky situation! Don't worry, you aren't alone in your troubles! Every girl at one time or another has to deal with this sort of stuff. It sounds like this guy really likes you. But there is one thing most guys don't like, and that's being cornered by more than one girl. He's probably just confused as to what to do. Talk to your friend and see if you can't find some common ground. She has a right to like him, same as you. If it means your friendship, think it over. You wouldn't want to ruin a good friendship over a guy, would you? Sit her down and see if you can maybe set her up with another guy or

JUST BECAUSE HE'S FAB

A lot of girls think that Prince William, Princess Diana's son, ROCKS. You can find out more about him through a page at his Dad's, the Prince of Wales, site.

http://www.princeofwales.gov .uk/gallery/william/index.html

maybe both agree to back off him and see what he wants to do. As for him, talk to him if you get the chance. Tell him you had fun with him and if he's interested you'd like to do it again some time. I wish you the best of luck!

— Lindsay, 16, Louisiana

Q. My new crush hates my best gal pal. What do I do?

—Anonymous, USA

1 I'd ask him why he dislikes her so much and tell him she's my pal no matter what. Get over it.

Mostly disagree   Somewhat disagree   Somewhat agree   Mostly agree

2 I'd ask her to "lay low" and steer clear of him at least for now.

Mostly disagree   Somewhat disagree   Somewhat agree   Mostly agree

3 I'd dump him. Friends are more important.

Mostly disagree   Somewhat disagree   Somewhat agree   Mostly agree

4 I'd put them together at a party or other activity and see if they could get along after all.

Mostly disagree   Somewhat disagree   Somewhat agree   Mostly agree

5 I'd tell him that I'll help her change so that he'll like her.

Mostly disagree   Somewhat disagree   Somewhat agree   Mostly agree

My Crush's Bud Is a Total Jerk!

The Problem Dear Boy-Zone: I have a major crush on this boy, Joe, and he is pretty nice to me, but he has this friend Bob who is a real jerk, and he is always being mean and teasing girls who like or go out with Joe. How should I handle my crush without making Bob totally humiliate me?

—Kyla, 14

A Solution Hey Kyla! You know Bob's doing this out of insecurity? He probably can't get dates as easily as Joe can. Some people think that it's best to ignore him, but that's not always the best or only way. You really should talk to Joe about this; it would be much easier on you if you tell him what's going on. Tell him (in private) that you really like him and want to go out with him. That's the hardest part. Then tell him that his friend Bob is really bugging you and that's why you hesitated to ask him out in the first place.

FEEL ROMANTIC?

Check out the Romantic Literature page. Keats, Shelley, Byron, Wordsworth, Gothic Literature, Jane Austin . . . complete books right here!

http://dept.english.upen n .edu/~mgamer/Romantic /index.html

FOLD PAPER AIRPLANES TOGETHER

Not boring, old-fashioned triangles. Show your sweetie the plans for a cruise missile, Delta Flyer, and Concorde. Not your father's paper airplane site!

http://koolpaperairplanes .hypermart.net/

Q. My boyfriend is a real hottie, and all the girls like him and flirt with him. What should I do to keep the girls away from my guy? What would you do if this were happening to you?

—Shayna, 13, Arizona

1 I'd do nothing about it. If he really liked me, it wouldn't matter if my friends flirt.

Mostly disagree   Somewhat disagree   Somewhat agree   Mostly agree

2 I'd make sure all the girls know for sure that he and I are exclusively dating.

Mostly disagree   Somewhat disagree   Somewhat agree   Mostly agree

3 I'd have a sleepover, invite all the girls who are flirting with my guy, and then ask them about their boyfriends. If they don't have any, I'd encourage them to chase someone else.

Mostly disagree   Somewhat disagree   Somewhat agree   Mostly agree

4 I'd try to match these girls up with some of my boyfriend's friends.

Mostly disagree   Somewhat disagree   Somewhat agree   Mostly agree

5 I'd ask my boyfriend how he feels about all the girls flirting with him.

Mostly disagree   Somewhat disagree   Somewhat agree   Mostly agree

If Joe feels the same way that you feel about him, and it sounds like he does, then he'll probably appreciate you telling him and just tell Bob to lay off. It's not as hard for guys to tell their friends to lay off for a while, as it is for us girls. It might be good to talk to Bob after you and Joe have a date. Tell him that you're sorry, but you knew he would antagonize you just for liking a guy! I hope this turns out okay. Have fun with Joe!

—Callan, 12, U.K.

GIFT IDEA

All you do is go into a place on your computer with pictures. For instance, I use "Creata Card." Take the pictures and paste them on the left side of the page. Next to each picture write something sweet, like "I'll tell you_____ all day!" Cut out each picture and phrase. Staple them all together and you have your own coupon book. Let your sweetie fill in the blanks.

My B.F. Said Something Insensitive. Now My Gal Pals Hate Him!

The Problem Dear BoyZone: After school some of my friends and I went into town with some lads from school. I had never liked this boy before, but he was so funny and cute and had views on everything, so I just couldn't resist him. We hung out for a couple of days, but then my best friend told them all that she had been attacked (which I already knew), but he made a joke of it because he thought she was joking. Now they have fallen out and I haven't seen him in ages. I'm stuck in the middle. HELP!!!!

—Jennifer, 13

A Solution

Hey Jennifer! It's always hard when you have to choose between your friends and a guy. But if they were really good friends, then they wouldn't make you choose. They would just accept that you like him and realize that it's your choice to pick a guy . . . they don't have to approve of him first. And hopefully you'll be lucky and they will realize how cool he is too. If he didn't know the "attack" was real and he made a joke, maybe if he talked to your friend and said he was sorry, and that he didn't mean to be so insensitive, she would forgive his mistake. But, beware; if he's the kind of guy who actually thinks that sort of horrible stuff IS funny, then you don't want to hang with him. If he's willing to apologize for the misunderstanding, he's a keeper!

—Rachael, 17, Florida

Knowing When to Confide

Knowing when to confide and who to confide in is the only way your confidences will be understood and respected. List the people here who you feel you could confide the worst situation to and still be loved and respected.

Falling In and Out of Love

First He's Mad, Then Says He Loves Me. Whazzup?

The Problem Dear BoyZone: There is a guy in my Geography class, and one minute he is mad at me and then next he says he loves me. Is he just trying to be annoying or does he really have some feelings for me? What would you do?

—Brittney, 14, Tennessee

A Solution Hey Brittney! If I were you, I'd just ignore him and see if he does it again. If he keeps it up, I'd either get one of my friends to confront him or I'd go up to him myself and ask him what's wrong. Ask him why is he being annoying, or just ask him, "Do you have feelings for me?" See if he wants to go out. He may be too shy to ask so he's just cutting up so you'll notice him. If you like him, it would be better to talk to him than for him to continue being annoying. He may have feelings for you, but he might also have a weird way of showing it.

—Kate, 12, Australia

First He Stares, Then He Ignores Me. Whazzup?

The Problem   Dear BoyZone: OK, there is this boy I really like . . . but how can I tell if he likes me? This boy will walk by me and give frequent stares or he'll just not look at me—you know, like try to avoid me. Are these a couple of signs he's interested in me? Is he afraid of me? Please, I hope you can answer my question.

—Erin, 16

WEB watch

SOMETHING FUN TO DO TOGETHER

Want to break the ice? Everyone loves comics! Snoopy, Dilbert, and lots more are right here.

http://www.comics.com

A Solution   Hey Erin! Boys act weird whether they like you or not. But they act really weird when they DO like you (*'cause they are nervous*). Why don't you just hint around to him that you like him and see how he reacts. If he seems proud or happy, then he likes you. Just ask him if he wants to hang out with you sometime. That would probably be the best idea. You could smile right at him next time he walks by and stares. Some guys will pick up on this and ask you out. If he's too shy, however, first you could ask him to a group activity, something where there will be other couples so he won't feel too pressured or freak out being alone with you all the time on a first date.

—Rachael, 17, Florida

He's Moving On, and I Want Him Back!

The Problem Dear Boy-Zone: My best friend is named Phil, and he is recently my ex-boyfriend. I love him to death, and I would do anything to have him back as my boyfriend. We know each other better than we know ourselves, but he wants to date the "prettier" girls (blonde XXX's), and I just want him back. Our friendship hasn't been the same since we broke up, and I can't lose him because I lost my other best friend when he committed suicide on his 15th birthday.

—Christine, 14

Say What You Mean; Mean What You Say

Imagine how different any hour of your life could be if everyone meant what they said. No one asking "How are you?" who didn't care about the answer. No silly recitations of "Well, so and so said this or that." Write about a time when you said something you didn't mean—or when someone said something they didn't mean to you. What happened next? Was the outcome positive? Close your eyes. Imagine yourself back at that time. Now speak your peace again. Remember, don't let yourself get tongue-tied or say things you don't mean. How was the outcome different in your imagination? Write about it here.

A Solution Hey Christine! Well, does he know you still feel this way about him? Tell him you want him back! Or maybe you should dye your hair blonde (just kidding!). How do you know he's after blondes? Did he say so? You should not change your appearance for anyone. Who says these girls are "prettier" anyway? Just let him know you are still there for him. He might try dating one of these girls and realize that you are the one he wants.

Seriously, talk to him or do a little "investigating." Find out which girl he likes. You may just have to outlast these girls. You two sound like a good pair of friends and a couple. Fate will take its course. I really hope you two stay friends or even better because you know each other inside and out like the back of your palms. (*Editor's note:* So sorry about your other friend who killed himself. Realize that if your ex-boyfriend dates someone else, it's certainly not as bad as committing suicide.) There may still be a future for you and your old b.f.

—Suzanne, 14, Florida

I Dumped Him.
Now I Want Him Back!

The Problem Dear BoyZone: I went out with this guy, then I made the mistake of dumping him. Now I like him more than ever. I asked for another chance and he said yes. After his relationship with his other girl, I'm gonna ask him out. Or should I

Time Travel

Things in life can change so much, so fast. Try this little experiment: First, write down what was going on in your life a year ago. Maybe you were in a different school or had a different set of friends than you do now. Now take the other side of the paper and write out what you would like your life to be like a year from now. Put the date on it and put it in a safe place—a shoebox in the closet or in your diary. When you take it out and read it in a year, see if things are getting closer to what you want, or further away. Then you will know what kind of changes you want to make. Your life is all yours, and only you can decide how to spend it. If you check on what you think is important at least once a year, it will help you make plans for the future.

just lay off and see if he asks me? Should I make the first move? Should I even go out with him again?

—Elizabeth, 14

A Solution   Hey Elizabeth! This is very confusing. I can only imagine how it is for you. First of all, I think that you both should sit down and talk to each other. Sort out both of your feelings for one another. I wouldn't push him into a relationship, especially when he is in one, and when and if he breaks up with this girl, you just might want to give him time. I mean, come on, would you want to start another relationship with someone else when you JUST got out of one?

See where both of you are when you think BOTH of you are ready before anyone makes a move. Really think about it because I am sure that you don't want feelings to get hurt, his or yours. If you feel that you are ready for the relationship, then I say go ahead and make the move.

And to your other question—Should you even go out with him again?—that is just something only you can decide. It is something once again that you have to sort out and think about. I hope this helps!

—Jen, 14, Washington, USA

"You Can Quote Me on That"

If only I could turn back time,
If only I had saved what I still had.
If only I could turn back time,
I would stay.
—From Aqua,
"Turn Back Time" (lyrics)
Submitted by
Aquagirl, 13, Idaho

Memories of a Broken Heart Are Ruining My New Relationship.

The Problem Dear BoyZone: I have been with my b/f for a week. I am pretty sure I am his first g/f, and he REALLY likes me; I just think maybe he is moving a little fast. Saturday night I realized that I don't really like him as much as I thought I did, but now I am starting to like him again. My friend said I just sound like I am afraid of falling in love because I don't want to get my heart broken again. And he is the first guy to actually show me how he feels, and it kinda scares me. I don't really know how to react to it. He is SO sweet, and I don't want to break his heart! How can I forget the old relationship that broke my heart and let this one stand on its own?

—Confused, 15

LOVE STAR WARS?

Some days do you feel like Han and Leia on the ice planet? You and your sweetheart can find out what character in *Star Wars* you are most like with this personality quiz! You'll find it at this site.

http://underwire.msn.com /underwire/social /millenium/58Millenium.asp

A Solution Hey "Confused"! I think your friend is right. You are afraid of falling in love, or even trusting another guy, because if you do, it will make you more vulnerable to getting your heart broken or getting let down. It's really OK to feel this, and trust me, you aren't alone. We will fall in and out of love many times in life, and we will get our hearts broken most of the time! But it's a learning experience. You are learning how to build your self-esteem so that eventually things like that won't knock you down.

As for the guy, you say you are his first girlfriend. Well, just like for us girls, there is no manual on how to react with someone of the opposite sex. There are plenty of guides, but they don't always suit someone's personality because everybody is different. It must be hard for him to know what you want and what you don't want.

Explain to him how you feel about this. Explain that you are not sure you are ready to make a deep commitment, and explain why. He sounds like the kind of guy who will understand, and he will slow down. And remember, you're a teenager, you're only young once, so just have fun. Don't get too attached if you're not ready and you won't get hurt.

—Lara, 14, Australia

I Love Him, but I'm Starting to Doubt Him.

The Problem Dear BoyZone: My boyfriend and I have been together for eight months, and I really love him. But I have a lot of doubts. I don't know if he's sincere about our relationship. I want to know if this is the first sign of a relationship going wrong, and what should I do about it?

—Jacqueline, 16

A Solution Hey Jacqueline! DON'T PANIC! There is no reason to believe that your relationship is going wrong at all! Everybody has doubts about things, but it doesn't necessarily mean those doubts are anything serious, or even true. Your boyfriend may be totally serious about your relationship! What leads you to believe he isn't? Before you go panicking that your

Journalize It!

Putting the Past Behind You

This is a fun way to leave old stuff behind and locate yourself firmly in the present tense. Get a piece of paper and write down whatever it is in the past that's bothering you. Be detailed and specific. Then at the bottom, write "All of this is over and I am free!" Then crumple it up in a ball and stand where you can toss it over your shoulder into a wastepaper basket. When you hear it hit the basket, you are free.

relationship is starting to go wrong, you should talk to your boyfriend about it. Tell him that you love him, but you are worried he is not sincere about your relationship. Ask him how he feels about it, and about you.

You two have been together for a long time, and you shouldn't let little doubts get in the way of it. If your boyfriend wasn't sincere about your relationship, then it probably wouldn't have lasted this long! Tell your boyfriend that you'd really like to know how he feels now. If he isn't sincere about the relationship, then maybe you two need to work at things a bit; but it doesn't mean your relationship is going wrong! If he is sincere about it, then that's OK, and you can just be happy knowing you've got the perfect boyfriend after all! Heaps of luck!!

—Shannon, 15, England

Well, everybody hurts sometimes; Everybody cries. And everybody hurts sometimes. And everybody hurts sometimes. So, hold on, hold on.
—From an R.E.M. song, "Everybody Hurts" Submitted by Adina, 13, Nebraska

I Was Cold. Now I Think He's a Hottie. Should I Tell Him?

The Problem Dear BoyZone: I like this boy I have known since primary school. We were friends in primary school, and I

Smiling Back at the Mirror

Of course, you want your guy to like you. But how much do you like you? When most of us look in the mirror, we are checking for flaws, like these: Is my hair combed? Do I have something stuck in my teeth? Is that a ZIT? Take one day, and every time you look in the mirror, say to yourself silently, I really like that girl. And smile. If you feel significantly different at the end of the day, do it for a week. Draw a picture of your smiling self right here. Then from now on, make it a habit to smile at yourself. After a while, you will notice that other people will smile at you more often.

My Smiling Self

believe that we would have been even more if I hadn't been so cold. In secondary school I still have a crush on him. Should I let him know my feelings, or do you think I have waited too long and now it's too late?

—Gina, 13, Barbados

A Solution   Hey Gina! Hi there! This guy—has he ever hinted to you that he likes you? If he hasn't, it could be that he's afraid. You let this guy go once, so don't let him go again. Tell him your feelings about everything. If he likes you, then great, wonderful! But if he just sees you as a friend, then, well, just move on. Telling him is much better than keeping it to yourself. At least you'd know the outcome without asking yourself "what if?" If you are warm and friendly now, he'll probably forget that you were cold in the past. It's worth a try. Anyway, good luck!

—Dani, 14, Malaysia

WEB watch

WONDERING HOW SMART YOU ARE?

Check out this online Intelligence Test. It's challenging, but fun!

http://cech.cesnet.cz/IQ /index.php

How Do You Survive Being Dumped?

Editor's note: Letters came in from a lot of girls about this one too.

A Solution

Hey, everybody. First of all, it's normal to feel sad when a boyfriend you care a lot about dumps you. It hurts. But now it's time to move on. Don't let yourself get depressed enough to think about suicide. Try not to think about him 24 hours a day. That will just make you feel worse!

WEB*watch*

HELP!

Blow it? Need an apology?
Check out the apology generator from the Karma Farm.

http://www.karmafarm.com
/formletter.html

Instead, go out and have some fun. Hang out with your girlfriends. Do anything to take your mind off him! Whenever you start to feel yourself think about him, gently but firmly pinch that little tab of skin between your thumb and your first finger. Don't worry; it doesn't really hurt! The reason for this is that the spot there is connected to a certain part of your brain, and when you give it a little pinch when you find yourself thinking about him, it starts you thinking about something else.

Good Luck! And don't worry, you'll find a really great guy someday!

—Julia S., Ontario, Canada

How Do You Break Up with a Guy? I Don't Want to Hurt Him.

The Problem

Many girls asked this question: How do I break up with a guy? I don't want to hurt him.

A Solution

To all who asked about this:

I don't know what's more nerve-wracking—asking someone out or facing them to break up with them. Probably the latter. You've got the right idea by not wanting to hurt him. Unfortunately, there's going to be a bit of "hurt" no matter what. Nobody likes feeling "rejected" or "unwanted," so I think what you need to do is tell him that this is not the case. You say he's a really great guy and all, so, first of all, make sure he knows that.

I can agree with those who don't want to use "the same old lines." They're so cliché that they have no meaning nowadays. Also, don't get someone else to do it for you. This can just cause more confusion and hurt than it's worth. For you it might be the "easy way out," but it's not necessarily the best.

Honestly, I think the truth is the best method here. Lots of people plan exactly what they're going to say in the breakup, but I think that's not the best thing. You should just sit down and tell him in a caring way how you feel and why it's not working. Try to create a mutual agreement about this rather than, "I'm dumping you." If you don't feel comfortable talking, write a long sincere letter with exactly how you feel. Don't hide your feelings, it can just make things worse, but don't be "brutally honest" either.

Best of luck!

—Meg B., 14, Ontario, Canada

Editor's Note: Because so many girls asked about this, we're adding comments from other B.Z. columnists, too.

❉ Lies are probably the worst thing to do in a breakup. If you tell someone, for example, "Oh, my parents aren't letting me date," and then they catch you out the next day with some guy, the friendship will go down the drain. Honesty IS the best policy.

❉ Guys deal with rejection differently than girls. They won't go running to their best friend crying, but the hurt

will be inside . . . maybe taken out in a basketball game or
something.

❊ Open discussions or letters are the best way to get across
your feelings. Even if the reaction doesn't seem the way you'd
react, sincerity WILL impact him on the inside. So keep
things open.

❊ Remember to think over your reason for breaking up and
if you're sure it's what you want to do. Make sure you have
reasons to explain your decision that don't offend or insult
the guy.

❊ "It's just not working." Why not? And are there perhaps
ways it COULD work, if you wanted it to? If not, then address this fact with compassion.

❊ Keeping the friendship is not as remote as it may seem, if
you TRULY want it to stay and aren't just "being nice." Being
too nice and saying things that you don't feel can mix up
things and cause confusion in the future, just as much as being
too harsh can be.

Boyfriend Trouble

I'm Torn Between Two Guys.

The Problem Dear BoyZone: A new guy that I think is really cute and smart asked me out, only so did someone else! Someone that I used to go with asked me. After we broke up the first time, we were still friends. Who should I go with?

—Julie, 14

A Solution Dear Julie: You're torn between two guys, and you want them both. There's Guy A, the cute and smart one, and Guy B, your friendly ex. They both want you, but you can only take one of them, so one's going to get hurt.

Some Solutions: The first thing is, why is your ex your ex? What went wrong? If he screwed up, chances are he will do the same thing again. You cannot (no matter how hard you try) change someone. It's good you're friends with your ex-boyfriend, but that can be against you if you go out with him. When you break up, chances are you may not be comfortable around him. I think you should go out with this new guy. His slate's clean. Remember, your ex will be hurt, so give him some space after you say you're not for him.

My best friend was recently in this situation. She turned them both down, so neither one got hurt. You may want to do this. I hope this works for you.

Good luck!

— Megan H., 11, Michigan, USA

Likes Me? Likes Me Not? It's Driving Me Crazy!

The Problem   This guy told my friend that he would like to get to know me, maybe be a little more than friends. The thing is we both are really shy. So it was hard for us to talk. So we didn't, except for the occasional "Hey, What's Up?" Then he tells his friend that he kind of likes this girl at his church, and he just wants to be friends with me. Now he talks to me more than he did when he supposedly liked me. Is he lying about the girl or what? Where does he stand, anyway?

— Lori, 17

A Solution   Hey Lori! You know him far better than I do, so there are probably a few possible answers to that depending on his personality. Either he is trying to take the pressure off him and the pressure off you. If he is shy and so are you, then he probably needs time to figure things out. He also might be making you jealous.

Remember that nobody has a manual on how to act around the opposite sex, so he's probably just as confused as you are right now. You most probably haven't informed him of how the relationship is going so he thinks you might not like him anymore.

What you should do is find out his phone number (if you haven't already gotten it) and call him. It's easier this way because guys feel generally uncomfortable about getting all "mushy" over you with their friends around, so he probably wouldn't want you to talk to him like that 'round him. It's also far easier to talk on the phone than in person.

Figure out what you will say beforehand, and then just ad lib. Tell him that you want to know where the relationship stands and if there is anything going on between you. Then ask him how he feels about this girl at his church and if what you've been hearing is true.

MY FIRST DATE

Put in a few words and experience the magic of your first date!

http://www.agirlsworld.com
/rachel/magic-story
/myfirdat.html

Talk for a while about what you want, and basically get your feelings out. It's hard, but you just have to say what you feel and mean it, and we'll see what happens from there. Either that or he might be playing games with you—telling you he likes you then generally ignoring you and saying that he likes someone else to confuse you even more. It's not fair on you, and if that's what you feel he's doing, he's not really worth it. Good luck!

—Lara, 14, Australia

Q. You see your best friend's boyfriend eating lunch with another girl. What would you do if this happened to you?

—Anonymous, USA

1 I'd tell my friend and let her decide what to do.

Mostly disagree   Somewhat disagree   Somewhat agree   Mostly agree

2 I'd confront him later and ask why he was eating with this girl.

Mostly disagree   Somewhat disagree   Somewhat agree   Mostly agree

3 I'd figure it was innocent or none of my business and just forget it.

Mostly disagree   Somewhat disagree   Somewhat agree   Mostly agree

4 I'd get the other girl alone and tell her that this guy belongs to my best friend and she'd better stay away from him.

Mostly disagree   Somewhat disagree   Somewhat agree   Mostly agree

5 I'd walk up to them during lunch and confront them both.

Mostly disagree   Somewhat disagree   Somewhat agree   Mostly agree

Journalize It!

Speaking Out

It's hard to be shy. You feel as if you can never say what you want to say. Start a confidence journal right here. Use this special box as a place to write down all the things you'd like to say out loud but can't. What would you like to speak out about? Draw a picture of the person you'd like to say something to but can't. Draw a word balloon, and write what you'd like to say. You might find that when you write it down, even if no one sees it, it feels as if you've gotten it off your chest.

Q. My boyfriend and I went on a field trip with our class. I overheard him telling his guy friends how "easy" I was. He doesn't know I heard him and is acting like nothing happened. What would you do? P.S. It's not true!

—Alicia, 14, Arizona

1 I'd tell him what I overheard and let him explain it for himself.

Mostly disagree   Somewhat disagree   Somewhat agree   Mostly agree

2 I'd have a friend ask him what's up and then have my friend tell me.

Mostly disagree   Somewhat disagree   Somewhat agree   Mostly agree

3 I wouldn't say anything.

Mostly disagree   Somewhat disagree   Somewhat agree   Mostly agree

4 I'd break up with him. He's not worth it if he is spreading rumors.

Mostly disagree   Somewhat disagree   Somewhat agree   Mostly agree

5 I'd ask one of his friends what's up and why my about-to-be-ex-boyfriend is saying that about me. It's not cool to talk about girls that way.

Mostly disagree   Somewhat disagree   Somewhat agree   Mostly agree

My B.F. Is Oversensitive and Controlling!

The Problem I am getting fed up with my boyfriend. He is so oversensitive; it is driving my other friends and me nuts. If we do one little thing he doesn't like, he'll ignore us for days and sometimes makes others stop talking to us. He gets mad at me if I am having a fight with someone else or talk to someone he's mad at. Is there any way to change this? He's a good person, but his habits are driving us wild.

—Jane, 13

A Solution Hey Jane! I have had a friend like that too. It can be very annoying. You have to deal with it. Could just be a stage, or he is just a moody person. I know how you feel—like you are walking on eggshells around him. Even though he gets upset when you mention the subject, just ask him flat out, "Are you okay? Because I worry about you and care." Tell him to just chill out and relax. He doesn't have to get so upset all the time. If he cares for you, he will understand why you are saying these things.

If this does not help, and he just becomes even worse, talk to his mom and dad if you know them well. Just ask if they have noticed his moods and if they are worried about him like you are. You may

ROBOTICS

Are you and your guy BORED? Come play with a robot thanks to San Jose, California's, Tech Museum of Innovation. You can control your own, thanks to a Shockwave program.

http://www.thetech.org
/robotics/

Q. I had a theme party and just invited girlfriends. Some of the girls were cool but others made fun of me because I didn't invite any guys. I felt like a dork. What would you do if this happened to you?

—Nancy, 13, New Zealand

1 Next time, I'd make it clear to all the girls coming that it's a "girls only" party so they wouldn't expect boys to be there.

Mostly disagree　　Somewhat disagree　　Somewhat agree　　Mostly agree

2 I'd tell the girls who made fun that they can have any kind of parties they want. They came to my party so they should have been polite.

Mostly disagree　　Somewhat disagree　　Somewhat agree　　Mostly agree

3 I'd have another party, invite boys but don't invite the girls who made fun of me.

Mostly disagree　　Somewhat disagree　　Somewhat agree　　Mostly agree

4 These girls are rude. I just wouldn't hang with them.

Mostly disagree　　Somewhat disagree　　Somewhat agree　　Mostly agree

5 I'd have another party and tell each girl to bring a boy she likes.

Mostly disagree　　Somewhat disagree　　Somewhat agree　　Mostly agree

not be worried about him, but you should because he may have a hard time dealing with his anger. I hope he doesn't and that it is just a stage. I hope I have helped you.

—Suzanne, 14, Florida

He's Older and in College. Should I Go with Him?

The Problem I went with a guy somewhere, and we both ended up telling each other that we liked each other. But there are three major problems. 1. He is going to college. 2. He is rooming with my cousin (it would be kinda weird for him). 3. He is 19 and I am 15. What should I do? Go for it or just forget about it?

—Jessica, 15

A Solution Hey Jessica! Well, first of all you should think seriously about this boy before you make any decisions! OK, so there may be some hassles involved, but is this guy worth all the trouble? He may well be, and you'll know straight away if the answer is yes. It all depends on just how much you want this boy!

The only major problem I can see here is the obvious age difference. You two have totally different lifestyles; you are still at school while this guy is going to college and could get a job any time he wanted. You should decide if you can handle this. The fact that he shares a room with your cousin may be difficult, but it's not the end of the world.

All of these problems can be overcome if you are both willing to work at it enough. If you decide that you really like this boy, then you are lucky! It can be very hard to find a guy you like and who likes you back! If you like him that much, then you should go for it! There is quite a big age gap that may be weird, and it might not even work out, but stranger things have happened!

Do you want to stand around thinking "what if?" or get out there, do something about your feelings, and make a go at this relationship? BUT REMEMBER, if you do decide to go for it, then you should do things properly!!

Explain the situation to your parents, first of all. They may be shocked at the age of the boy you want to go out with, but they need to know what's going on because this is not just the usual girlfriend-boyfriend situation. He is a whole four years older than you! Get him to agree to meet your parents. Also, remember your limits and values and stick to them! Just because he is older than you, DO NOT let him push you around! Good luck!

—Shannon, 15, England

My B.F. Is a Dork Fashion Plate!

The Problem My B.F. wears every new clothes and hair fad that comes out! Some of them look okay on him, but others make him look like super-dork! How can I get him to stop doing this and just be himself?

—Laura, 16

A Solution

Hey Laura! I think that you should just tell him that he shouldn't try to be like other people and just be how he wants to be, not someone else. Try to keep his feelings in mind. I mean, you don't want to cause an argument; it could just lead to a breakup, and who wants that?! If you think that he would take the news a little bit too hard, then tell a friend of his, and then maybe he will get your boyfriend to change his mind about all these styles. Don't tell someone who will make him only feel bad about this, tell someone you can trust to get the point across but will be gentle about it. Hope this helps! Remember one thing: Communication is an important thing in a relationship!

—Jen, 14, Washington

An Older Boy Got Too "Touchy-Feely."

The Problem

Dear BoyZone: I recently moved, but in my old town there was this boy who was a sophomore, and I am an 8th grader. I was at a softball game and he was massaging my back. Well, he is a very popular boy, and most of the girls in my high school would die to go out with him (it's 7th to 12th grades here). He has a girlfriend, but he was massaging my back and going up my shirt and touching me where I didn't want him to. I didn't do anything about it because I figured he would think I was a big baby and also that he would tell all the others sophomores about me too! I wanted to tell his girl-friend, but I never got a chance to before I moved. She is a jun-ior, and her sister is one grade above me and is like my best

Fashion Fun

Is it better to try out new fashions all the time, or better to have a "look" that you stay with? If you've ever seen the "Paris Premiere" on any fashion collection, you'll probably agree that those clothes don't look like ANYBODY could wear them. Take some clothes out, enough to make an "outfit," and lay them out on the bed or the floor. Then take out a fashion magazine (appropriate to your age) and tear out some pictures of "their" outfits. Which looks more like you? Which do you like better? See if adding a little something (a hat, a necklace, a scarf) might make your outfit seem more "fashionable." Cut and paste your new look here.

friend. What should I do? Should I just leave it a "what's done is done" kind of thing, or should I tell her?

—Tracy, 13, Florida

A Solution Hey Tracy! It looks like even though this guy is popular, he's a real creep. No one, not a single person on the face of the earth has the right to touch you when you don't want them to! Never let someone take advantage of you because you are afraid they will view you as a baby. You aren't a baby; you are a human being, and your body is yours, so you decide who is allowed to touch you.

Don't be afraid to talk to someone. Talk to a school counselor or your parents. Just because you moved doesn't mean everything is okay now. Talk to your friend and try to clue in her sister on what a creep this guy is. She deserves to know, and you deserve to live with a clear conscience. My suggestion is to talk to an adult first. Your parents won't get angry; they may be upset because this happened, but they won't be mad at you. Don't keep this to yourself. Talk to someone A.S.A.P. and let the cat out of the bag on this guy before he starts "touching" someone else! I hope this helps you! Good Luck, and remember: You are in charge of you!

—Lindsay, 16, Louisiana

My Guy Is Smothering Me!

The Problem Dear BoyZone: My boyfriend is scaring me by being too "into me." I like him, but that keeps me away to a certain point. We spend the right amount of time together, but he's too

Q. All the boys in my age group at school are dirty, sloppy, and like to wear wrinkled clothes. How do my friends and I get through to them to clean up their acts? What would you do if this happened to you?

— Anonymous, USA

1 I'd set a good, neat example and hope they'll catch on.

Mostly disagree   Somewhat disagree   Somewhat agree   Mostly agree

2 I'd pick a day and dress just like they do and see how they like it.

Mostly disagree   Somewhat disagree   Somewhat agree   Mostly agree

3 I'd cut out pictures of "dapper," "stylin'" guys from magazines and slip them into the guys' lockers.

Mostly disagree   Somewhat disagree   Somewhat agree   Mostly agree

4 I'd tell one of them that I trusted to pass the word to the others; they either clean up or go "dateless."

Mostly disagree   Somewhat disagree   Somewhat agree   Mostly agree

5 I'd have my mom tell their moms.

Mostly disagree   Somewhat disagree   Somewhat agree   Mostly agree

good to me and too sweet to be true. He's smothering me, and it's scary to a certain extent. I told him, and he felt it was a one-sided relationship anyway. How can I change or fix our differences?

— Daria, 16

A Solution

Hey Daria! It looks like you have a lot of mixed emotions on this. You like him so you push him away. He is good to you and it scares you. You said you two talked about it and his response wasn't all that sweet. I have had a boyfriend like that. He was way possessive; it was like he always had to let everyone know that I belonged to him. As soon as I said something, he said, "Fine. I just won't even sit by you." Now that hurt. I had seen him do that to other girls and they cowered and said, "No, I'm sorry. I want you to be with me." So what did I do? I simply said that if he really loved me, he would back off and we could work this out.

> **WEB**watch
>
> **DISCOVER YOUR LOVE TYPE**
> Lovetypes: an online personality quiz.
>
> http://www.starr-rhapsody.com
> /lovetypes/lovetypes.html

He, of course, gave me a huge guilt trip and tried to make me feel like I was being selfish. But with the help of all of my girl-friends, I didn't give in and we broke up. I don't think you can change the way he is unless you two are really in love. You said he was too good to be true; well, let's hope that all that sweetness will help you two work it out. Just talk, and get support from family and friends. It could work out, but be careful! If he makes you feel like it's your fault and you don't love him back, shake him off and move on. Hope it all works out for you!

—Lindsay, 14, Louisiana

A Place for Space

Are there too many people in your world? Parents, siblings, friends, boyfriend, teachers, coaches, church members? Do you ever get to spend an hour by yourself? See if you can take just an hour and be really alone. Do you enjoy your own company? What do you think about when there's no one else around? Remember, you are the only person who will always be with you, from cradle to grave. Take some time out from the crowd, and get to know yourself. Write about what you did and how it felt to be alone for that hour.

Q. My crush and I are about to break up because I'm friends with a girl he hates. What would you do if this happened to you?

— Darla, 16, New Mexico

1 I'd just make sure that I didn't put the two of them together. He should back off on his position.

Mostly disagree   Somewhat disagree   Somewhat agree   Mostly agree

2 I'd tell him that he doesn't control who I am friends with. I wouldn't expect him to like her, but I AM going to stay friends with her.

Mostly disagree   Somewhat disagree   Somewhat agree   Mostly agree

3 I'd try to get to the bottom of the problem. I'd ask him exactly why he doesn't like her and try to talk him out of his feelings.

Mostly disagree   Somewhat disagree   Somewhat agree   Mostly agree

4 I'd get the two of them together for a confrontation. They work it out, or I drop him.

Mostly disagree   Somewhat disagree   Somewhat agree   Mostly agree

5 I'd ask her why he doesn't like her and ask her to make an extra effort to be friendly to him.

Mostly disagree   Somewhat disagree   Somewhat agree   Mostly agree

When He's with His Pals, I Get the Cold Shoulder!

The Problem   Why is it when you are alone with a guy, he talks the sweetest he can to you, then as soon as he gets around his friends he is totally different? It's like he doesn't even think of me as his girl; that's how rude he is. Why is that, and what can I do about it?

—Angela, 16

A Solution   Hey Angela! Guys are so weird and complicated. He wants you to like him, so he acts sweet to you. But on the other hand, his ego gets in the way, and he wants his friends to like him too, so he tries to act all macho and cool when they are around. My advice is to just ignore him when he is around his friends 'cause he probably doesn't mean to act that way.

Or you could just try to work things out where you aren't around him at the same time he is around his friends. You could also get to know the girlfriends of his pals and see if they feel the same way about how they are treated. If you all feel "ignored," then you can tell the guys how you feel. You don't expect them to get all "mushy" when they are with their friends, but they

Being deeply loved by someone gives you strength.

—Lao-Tzu
Submitted by
Aarika, 13, Washington

could at least not act like you don't exist. Give it a try. Girl Power!

—Rachael, 17, Florida

He "Bad-Mouths" Me to His Friends!

The Problem Dear Boy-Zone: You're at the pool. There's a total hunk who seems really interested in you. You walk up to him and he says something so totally rude and insulting to his friend, who's sitting next to him, about YOU! What would you do?

—Emili, 9

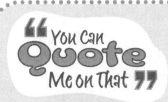

Don't speak.
I know just what
you're saying
So please stop explaining.
Don't tell me 'cause
it hurts

—From a No Doubt song,
"Don't Speak"
Submitted by
Dannica, 11, USA

A Solution Hey Emili! You can think I'm conservative, but I think that girls your age shouldn't think so much about guys since any boy-girl relationship will most probably not work out. Most guys your age still hate girls! But sometimes when a guy says something bad about a girl (I stress the word sometimes), it means that he likes her but doesn't want to lose "face" with his friends. When his buddies aren't around, you could go up to him and make friends and see what happens then. Good Luck!

—Dani, 14, Malaysia

He's My Best Girlfriend's Guy!

The Problem I don't have a boyfriend, and the boy I like is my best friend's guy. I didn't flirt or anything, but he asked me to be his girlfriend! I said no, but I really like him. This is a mess. Help!

—Monica, 13

A Solution Hey Monica! Well, is he definitely "going" with your friend exclusively? Because if he is, I would not mess with any of it and would try to find someone else. Find out from your friend if they have broken up. How does she feel about him now? If he is "free," he clearly likes you and you like him. Talk to him. The important thing is be yourself. I know that sometimes when girls are around guys, we get a little excited and don't want to be who we are, and usually guys like girls for who they are.

Tell him that you like him too. I mean you do, don't you? Tell him at the time you were confused about his relationship with your friend. If he really does like you, he will understand what you were going through. Try not to talk to him around a lot of people. Guys sometimes have BIG egos, and they hide their feelings when around a lot of people. Hope everything works out!

—Jen, 14, Washington

Boyfriends on the Internet

We Were Online Buds. Now I Want to Be Closer!

The Problem Dear BoyZone: I am friends with this guy, and I think, at one point, he liked me enough to ask me out, but we haven't talked in a few months. We used to talk online a lot, but now he is never on. I want to call him, but I don't know what to talk about or how to let him know that I want to be closer friends. Please give me some suggestions!

—Emily, 15, Wisconsin

A Solution Hey Emily! Don't stress over this guy's mood swings. It's just how guys are. And besides, guys are better as friends right now anyhow, but I can understand how you feel. You want him to be the kind of guy who will take you to the dance if no one else is free, right? Well, here are some suggestions that have worked for me in the past. Give them a try; what have you got to lose?

1. *Keep him talking.* Number one thing to remember about guys is they love to talk (some as much as girls!), so strike up a conversation about anything. Ask him if the football team won last Friday or what homework is in Geometry.

2. *Smile.* Once he is chatting away, keep a constant smile. Some girls call it flirting, but you will be surprised at the reaction he'll give you. Isn't it easier to talk to a smiling person than a person with no expression at all?

3. *Don't flood him with your gal pals.* Another point to remember: Nothing turns a guy off faster than a bunch of giggling girls drowning him. It's okay to bring your gal pals with you to talk to him (P.S.: Don't ditch the gals for the guys!), but you don't need the whole gang there.

4. *Invite him places.* Once you can hold a conversation with him longer than two minutes, ask him if he wants to go bowling as a friend thing. Or walk the mall. Hey, anything will work. Tell him to bring a friend for your friend, of course. Nothing will make the sparks fly faster than playing matchmaker with him.

Well, Emily, I hope these help. Good Luck and Go Get Him!
—Lindsay, 15, Louisiana

I see you—the only one who knew me,
And now your eyes see through me.
I guess I was wrong
So what now? It's plain to see we're over,
And I hate when things are over,
When so much is left undone.
—From "Deep Blue Something,"
Breakfast at Tiffany's (lyrics)
Submitted by
Jayne, 15, Oregon

Q. I like my best friend's boyfriend and she knows it. I never make any moves on him, but it's like she punishing me. She always tells me all about what they did on their dates, how much he loves her, etc. How can I get her to stop torturing me? What would you do?

—Zeta, 15, South Africa

1 I'd change the subject every time she does this. After a while she should get the hint.

Mostly disagree   Somewhat disagree   Somewhat agree   Mostly agree

2 I'd tell her that what she's doing is really hurting me; she knows it and she has to stop.

Mostly disagree   Somewhat disagree   Somewhat agree   Mostly agree

3 I'd assume that maybe she doesn't realize it hurts me. Then I'd remind her that I like this guy too.

Mostly disagree   Somewhat disagree   Somewhat agree   Mostly agree

4 If I were her best friend, then I'd assume that maybe she has no other gal-pals to talk to about him. So I'd just listen, even if it hurt.

Mostly disagree   Somewhat disagree   Somewhat agree   Mostly agree

5 I'd really make an effort to get a guy of my own, then I could chatter to her about HIM!

Mostly disagree   Somewhat disagree   Somewhat agree   Mostly agree

I Thought I Was E-Chatting with My Crush; It Was His Friend!

The Problem   Dear BoyZone: Internet Mess! There's this boy that I went out with for three or four months, and he treated me terribly! He would make fun of me and told me I was fat, ugly, and stupid. So he finally dumped me. The other night we started talking online. First he asked me to go out with one of his friends, and I said no. All of a sudden he asked me if I would go to a movie with him Friday. He started saying how sorry he was and how he wants me back. I didn't buy that it was him and so I asked him a question only he would know and he knew it. So I was pretty sure that it was him. He got back on saying he didn't want to go out. He'd been watching TV while his friend was online using his name! Should I be mad at him or his friend? Should this stop me from wanting to go back out with him?

—Jacque, 13, Iowa

A Solution   Hey Jacque! You should be mad at his friend, and so should he! He betrayed his trust and was really mean to you, and if you didn't find out, you'd be mad at the wrong guy. You have to decide if you believe him or if maybe he was lying and it was him just rubbing off a bad mood, only pretending that his friend was there using his name!! If this guy made the whole thing up, then forget the loser; he's not worth it. You don't need a "game-player" like that. (*Editor's note:* Remember, this guy treated you "terribly" and called you "fat, ugly, and stupid"!) But it could have been the friend, as he told you. I'd say talk to the old boyfriend face to face and ask if he's ready to go out with you again and treat you with the respect you deserve. If not, you don't need the abuse! Or try being friends with him first and see how it works out. Keep your self-esteem! Good luck!

—Zara, 12, England

He's a Net Chat Romeo, But Does He Really Like Me?

The Problem Dear BoyZone: I keep on talking to this guy on the computer. He tells me he likes me, and I don't know if he really means it or not because whenever I see him in person, he acts totally different around me. How do I get him to tell me if he really likes me or if he just wants to joke around on the computer?

—Jane, 13

A Solution Hey Jane! One of the great things about the Internet is that it lets us be whoever we want to be. If we are 3' 7" with hair the color of mud in real life, no one can prove otherwise if we say we are 5' 8" with blonde hair down to our ankles. Apart from changing what we look like, we can also change our personalities. I have occasionally bumped into friends from school on the Internet, and they are all totally different from how they are normally. The really loud and flirty ones at school are nearly always those who hide in the virtual corner of the chatroom without saying anything, while the people who I know as being the shy-and-retiring types become bubbly, talkative flirts.

It may be the same with the boy you have met. Although he may be funny and talkative and likes you when you are

DEDICATED TO THE ONE I LOVE

Declare your feelings in this dedication page. They're posted every Valentine's Day.

http://www.agirlsworld.com /amy/pajama/valentines /dedications-form.html

someone he Netchats to without having to meet, he may be just very shy in real life. The thing about talking to someone who you like in real (not virtual) life is that things normally go very slowly. You can tell what people think of you by how they react to what you tell them. On the Internet you can only know what someone is thinking by what they tell you.

Because of this, he may be wary of you, as he may not know if you like him. Meeting someone you've talked to on the Internet is kinda like starting on the 10th or 11th date. He may know lots about you, but he is probably finding it hard to take it all in at once. This, added to the fact that you exist in real life, as well as in lines of type on his screen, is probably making him feel a little unsure of what he's dealing with. The simple thing to do is to ask him—whether it's on- or offline—where you stand. He may not really know (boys can be such idiots, sometimes!), but it's worth a shot.

Even if he only wants to have fun on the Internet, you have to admit that you're probably having fun as well. Odds are that he's a bit shy without his keyboard, and unless you're really desperate to go out with him offline, as well, there's no harm in slowing everything down a bit—at least until he realizes that he can't live without you and must see you that instant. It may take a while (boys can be sooo slow), but what really counts is that you know that he does like you for your personality. If he only liked you when you were on his arm looking great, then you'd be in much bigger trouble.

—Janie, 15, England

Q. My boyfriend and I broke up because he is too shy. One day he said we'd better just be friends. That is three or four months ago, but I still can't get rid of him. What would you do if this was happening to you?

—Yuyusuke, 14, Thailand

1 I'd tell him I want to be friends, but he shouldn't stick to me like glue.

Mostly disagree   Somewhat disagree   Somewhat agree   Mostly agree

2 I'd ask him if he is SURE he doesn't want me for a girlfriend?

Mostly disagree   Somewhat disagree   Somewhat agree   Mostly agree

3 I'd just get a new boyfriend I like to spend time with. Then my old boyfriend would have to get the hint. Right?

Mostly disagree   Somewhat disagree   Somewhat agree   Mostly agree

He's Switching Schools! Will We Drift Apart?

Dear BoyZone: I like this hunk from my primary school and he gave me stars on my 10th and 11th birthday; and on my 12th birthday, he sent me a lovely bookmark and a card that has a very romantic poem written by him as well. He even bought me lunch on my 13th birthday! Now, we are in different schools, and I wonder if we are going to drift apart. What can I do to keep this guy interested?

—Evelyn, 13

A Solution   Hey Evelyn! Does he have a brother? (Just kidding!) Seems really nice, so I see no reason for you to have to try to keep him interested. Do you have his e-mail address? Phone number? Mailing address? Contact him and talk to him about things and hint about how you really miss him now that he's at a different school. I think letters really do it. Send him cute stationary and little bookmarks and stuff in the envelopes (and casually ask him if he has a girlfriend :o). You may drift apart, but if you love something and let it go, and it shows any signs of replying or coming back, then that's love. Don't be disappointed if he doesn't want to be with you; it's hard to keep a long-distance relationship. On the other hand, if he lives nearby, get a group

INTO NARNIA

Step into the fantastic world of Narnia together. Find out about the chronicles, meet the characters, and discover the author of this fabulous world.

http://www.narnia.com/

of friends to come along with you and hang out somewhere so it's not too awkward when you talk to him. Good luck!

—Tiffany, 11, Canada

My Online "Hottie" Went Cold!

The Problem Dear BoyZone: Help! I had a great e-mail "flirt" going with a guy for months (we exchanged pictures at the beginning). It's been great fun, and we were talking about meeting (he brought it up first). Now all he sends me are "forwards" like chain letters and jokes . . . nothing personal. What should I do?

—Daria, 13

A Solution Hey Daria! I've been in the same situation; it's quite frustrating indeed! I suggest you send him a short e-mail asking what's up and how come he didn't write anything personal for so long. Keep it short because it's possible he's just got less time to write. If that doesn't work, you could try sending him one of those cute e-cards saying you'd like to hear from him (www.bluemountain.com has some great ones). Ask if you are still on for meeting someday (as long as it's

You Can Quote Me on That

Love builds bridges where there are none.

—Delaney
Submitted by
Emilie, 10, USA

Q. I have been very mean to my American pen pal. I told him I wanted to be his girlfriend for a laugh to see what he'd say, but he said yes, and I haven't written back yet because I don't know what to say. I want to be his friend. What would you do if this were happening to you?

—Joan, 12, Ireland

1 I'd just write him and tell him I was kidding. Ooops! Sounds like we'd be living too far apart to be a real couple.

    Mostly disagree   Somewhat disagree   Somewhat agree   Mostly agree

2 I'd just be his long-distance, pen pal girlfriend. What can it hurt?

    Mostly disagree   Somewhat disagree   Somewhat agree   Mostly agree

3 I'd write and tell him I thought about it and I like him but just want to be friends.

    Mostly disagree   Somewhat disagree   Somewhat agree   Mostly agree

4 I'd write him and apologize. I'd ask him to still be my friend.

    Mostly disagree   Somewhat disagree   Somewhat agree   Mostly agree

5 I'd write him and say that I already have a boyfriend.

    Mostly disagree   Somewhat disagree   Somewhat agree   Mostly agree

in a "safe" public place and your parents say yes first and help make the arrangements and you go with a friend so you can make sure this guy is really who he says he is). If he doesn't react and keeps sending you boring chain letters, look for a new guy to talk to. Good luck!

—Tamira, 15, Belgium

My Summer Romance Went Home, and I'm Blue!

The Problem Dear BoyZone: Sicilia says: See I have a boyfriend and he is from California and I'm in Indiana. I just met him and he went back to California and I won't be able to see him till next summer and I really miss him. I don't even have his address. What should I do?

And from Mia: I just went on vacation and met this really great guy. We got really close and I basically felt like I was falling in love. Unfortunately, our vacation ended and we had to break up. It's been a week now, and every day I am still crying and feeling really depressed. Help, I need some advice on how to cope with losing him.

—Sicilia, 13, and Mia, 14

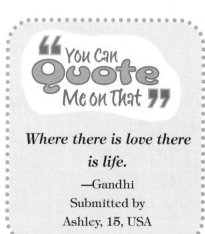

"You Can Quote Me on That"

Where there is love there is life.

—Gandhi
Submitted by
Ashley, 15, USA

Q. I have a boyfriend, but I feel we don't talk enough. When we do, my friends always start butting in and talking to him instead. What would you do if this were happening to you?

—Angel, 11, New Zealand

1 I'd talk to my friends when he's not around and let them know I need some time alone with my boyfriend.

Mostly disagree   Somewhat disagree   Somewhat agree   Mostly agree

2 Next time my guy and I are out, I'd make sure we were alone and just start a conversation.

Mostly disagree   Somewhat disagree   Somewhat agree   Mostly agree

3 Next time my friends started butting in, I'd just say, "Excuse me, but _____ and I were talking."

Mostly disagree   Somewhat disagree   Somewhat agree   Mostly agree

4 I'd let my friends yak away but make sure my guy and I are alone for a chat later.

Mostly disagree   Somewhat disagree   Somewhat agree   Mostly agree

5 I'd tell my boyfriend exactly how I felt. We don't talk enough, and I want to schedule some personal chat time with him.

Mostly disagree   Somewhat disagree   Somewhat agree   Mostly agree

A Solution

Hey Sicilia and Mia! It's hard to love a guy who's about 5000 miles away from you. It must be a tough time getting over this. Write and call him as soon as you can. Keep in touch; that way you'll never lose each other. Sicilia, do you have any info on this guy? If you can get one piece of info, maybe you can use one of the Internet "people search" services to at least get his e-mail. Sometimes first and last name only will get results. Let everything loose, and always know that if he does really care, then his spirit is right beside you. If writing and e-mailing isn't enough to keep you together, then sometime around the corner you might meet a new romance. But first you have to take time and think about how to get over him. I haven't had much experience with boys, but maybe you should keep him off your mind a little, but don't completely forget about him. Try playing extracurricular activities at school. Make new friends. Spend more time with your parents and siblings. Try to talk about this with a best friend. You'll feel much better when you express yourself.

—Tiffany, 11 Canada

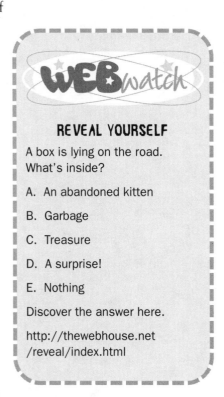

REVEAL YOURSELF

A box is lying on the road. What's inside?

A. An abandoned kitten

B. Garbage

C. Treasure

D. A surprise!

E. Nothing

Discover the answer here.

http://thewebhouse.net/reveal/index.html

Believe It or Not

I Look More Like a "Woman." Now He's Scared of Me!

The Problem Dear BoyZone: My boyfriend and I have gone out for two years. Everything was fine until I started maturing and wearing a little makeup and looking like an older female! Now he acts like I'm from Venus, and he's scared to even hold my hand. What's with this, and how can I fix it?

—Leda, 14

A Solution Hey Leda! You are about my age, and I started wearing makeup when I was 12. From what I hear about teenage guys, so far, more than half of them prefer girls in their natural look instead of makeup. But we girls don't think we look good without it. But whose decision should it really be? Ours, of course. And if he has a problem with that, then he's not a good boyfriend. Besides, who is he—your boyfriend or your parent? Guys should have some say in it, but they can't act the

Face Games

This works best with one friend, a couple of hand mirrors, and a bunch of makeup. (Makeup can be expensive, so see if there are some half-used things or colors that no one wanted in your mom's or sister's stuff. Ask! Don't just take!) Get some time and get your friend ready; wash faces, pin hair back. Then try to put on as much makeup as you can. Put on mascara and eyeliner and eye shadow and foundation and blush and lipstick and lip gloss and everything else you can think of! Just layer it over, put on lots and lots. Now show each other how you look (you'll probably be laughing by now). Now think about why some women wear all that makeup every day. Wash your faces (be careful not to get makeup all over the towels!) and look at how pretty you are without all that stuff. If you want, pick out one thing, like lipstick or mascara, and see if wearing just a little bit makes you feel pretty.

A famous beautician once said that if you are wearing makeup properly, no one will know that you are wearing any!

Fun? Now draw a picture here of the face you just discovered. The real you is beautiful!

The Beautiful Real Me!

way he does. You should talk to him, and if he still disagrees, then don't stay with him. He doesn't care, obviously. But if he says he's scared that other guys might be trying to hit on you 'cause you look older, reassure him and tell him that he is the only one for you and he shouldn't worry.

(*Editor's Note:* Also, if your boyfriend is your age, he might be shy and feel uncomfortable because you are looking like a "woman.")

When he started dating you, you were a "girl." This whole "woman" thing can put young guys in a nervous spin, so be kind to him. You guys are a couple and you should be comfortable talking to each other about your feelings, so go for it. Good luck!!!

—Angie, 14, Washington

WEB watch

WHAT'S THE SHAPE OF YOUR RELATIONSHIP?

Here's a fun quiz that asks you to pick different shapes you like.

Discover what kind of feelings you're experiencing today. We hope that you're playful, cheerful, and spontaneous!

http://users.rcn.com/zang .interport/personality.html

What Do You Do When You Like Two Brothers?

The Problem Dear BoyZone: I'm confused. I like two brothers at the same time. What do I do?

—Confused and Anonymous, USA

Q. How do you express your feelings to your boyfriend when you do not like him anymore and want to break up? What would you do if this were happening to you?

—Cassandra, 16, Nicaragua

1 I'd be alone with him and then tell him how I felt. I'd be gentle and just say I don't feel the same way I used to feel about him. The truth is best.

Mostly disagree   Somewhat disagree   Somewhat agree   Mostly agree

2 I'd start dating another guy so he'd get the hint.

Mostly disagree   Somewhat disagree   Somewhat agree   Mostly agree

3 I'd tell one of his friends and ask them to tell him.

Mostly disagree   Somewhat disagree   Somewhat agree   Mostly agree

4 I'd write him a really kind letter or e-mail breaking it off.

Mostly disagree   Somewhat disagree   Somewhat agree   Mostly agree

5 I'd try to get him interested in another girl so he'd break it off with me.

Mostly disagree   Somewhat disagree   Somewhat agree   Mostly agree

A Solution

Dear Confused: Oh boy! This is bad! You really need to get things straightened out FAST! It would be bad if this situation broke their brother/brother relationship up. You seriously need to talk to BOTH of them at the same time and let them know what's going on. If you don't let them know what's going on, then you could get a bad reputation if they found out that you were cheating and then passed it along to other guys!!!! There's no way that you could just dump one of them, or even both of them for that matter, and think that they won't find out. They eventually would.

So you need to talk to them. Tell them the situation. You like both of them, and there's no way that you could ever choose one over the other. They are both great guys. So instead of picking one, you could all be friends, and maybe then you could get another boyfriend with no brothers to worry about! And, of course, don't forget to tell them that you didn't intend on hurting either of them. If that's not how you feel, then don't listen to me. I'm just a girl trying to help a fellow teen that is as stressed out as me sometimes. Whatever you do, don't lie! Say it from your heart! Hope everything works out for you!

—Chelsea F., 12, Nevada

"You Can quote Me On That"

I'll be your dream,
I'll be your wish,
I'll be your fantasy.
I'll be your hope,
I'll be your love,
be everything that
you need.
I'll love you more with
every breath
truly madly deeply do . . .
—From a Savage Garden song,
"Truly Madly Deeply"
Submitted by
Desiree, 13, Florida

Q. I'm going with a boy. I was at camp with his sister. He wrote his sis a letter and enclosed two letters that he wanted her to give to other girls! We opened them and he was asking these girls to go out with him! What would you do if this happened to you?

—Annie, 14, South Carolina

1 I'd confront him with his sister and the letters and ask him to explain himself!

Mostly disagree   Somewhat disagree   Somewhat agree   Mostly agree

2 I wouldn't say anything. I'd just dump him. Sure, it was wrong for me to open those letters, but it was also wrong for him to ask other girls out.

Mostly disagree   Somewhat disagree   Somewhat agree   Mostly agree

3 I'd confront him alone without the letters. I'd just pretend I didn't know anything but ask him if he still wants to go out with only me. If he lies and says yes, then I'd dump him.

Mostly disagree   Somewhat disagree   Somewhat agree   Mostly agree

4 I'd ask the sister to tell him she doesn't want to pass those letters on, and she thinks that if he's going with me, he shouldn't be sending letters to other girls.

Mostly disagree   Somewhat disagree   Somewhat agree   Mostly agree

5 I'd write letters to two of his friends and ask them to go out with me! See how he likes it!

Mostly disagree   Somewhat disagree   Somewhat agree   Mostly agree

He Prefers TV to Talking with Me!

The Problem Dear BoyZone: I need help. My boyfriend is so boring. We hardly ever do things together. We never talk about anything on the phone because everything I try to talk to him about he doesn't hear me because he has his nose stuck in the stupid TV. I really like him and need some advice on what to do to perk up conversation. Please help me!

—Ashley, 12, South Carolina

A Solution Hey Ashley! If you think your boyfriend's really boring and you guys don't do anything together, to me that would just sound like he's a regular boy-friend (not a BOY-FRIEND that you could get along with). If you want your relationship to work out and become stronger and healthier, go out and tell

GIFT FOR YOUR CRUSH

Just take a bunch of different variety of stickers, pictures, Valentines, or cut construction paper. Then glue or stick them onto an ordinary paper lunch sack. Stuff it with candy, punch a hole in the top, tie a ribbon through the hole, then give the bag to your friend or crush! I did it to my boyfriend and friends, and they loved them (especially all the candy I stuffed in the bags!!)!

—Ami, 13, Washington

him what you just told ME! You don't want to compete with the TV for his attention!

Be honest and gentle and say that you two never do anything exciting! You could go to the mall together, play games. Find out what his hobbies are. Ask his guy friends what he's into, then learn about it and bring it up in conversation. If it's a subject he's into, he'll probably really brighten up.

But I think the best way to perk up the conversation is when you're with FRIENDS. You're all relaxed and there isn't that awkward pause between sentences when you have nothing else to say. Invite some of his friends and some of your friends and get together and laugh and talk and do whatever you want. Maybe that will loosen him up and get him yapping until your ears fall off!

—Tiffany, 12, Canada

My Cousin Likes a Guy on Drugs.

The Problem   Dear BoyZone: My cousin met a guy at school that she likes a lot. Then he told her that he's involved with drugs. I think he could be lying 'cause he might think it's cool. I keep telling my cousin to get away from him, but she says she wants to help him first. If he really is doing this stuff or not, thinking it's cool, that is bad too. What should I do? She won't get away from him and wants to "help." If this is true, I'm afraid he might talk her into doing drugs too.

—R., 13

A Solution   Hey R.! This problem happens a lot to girls this age. All I can say is talk to your cousin; tell her that if she gets involved it might not turn out well. Tell her that you think it would be better if she stayed out of this boy's problem. Instead she could end up with a problem of her own. If she really likes him, she'll leave him alone or tell him that she likes him but just doesn't go out with boys who are into drugs.

I know it sounds weird, but you really need to talk to her. She has to take a stand. Either stay away from this guy or research some local teen drug treatment counseling centers and tell him to get into one. Tell her that you care for her very much and you don't want her to get hurt. Tell her that her life and health is more important than any guy.

—Kate, 12, Australia

Boys Flirt Then Ignore Me. What Now?

The Problem Dear BoyZone: Guys seem to have an off-and-on attitude about me. They flirt with me one day, and the next day they totally blow me off. Am I doing something wrong? Why are they doing it? Thanks for taking the time to read this!

—Ellie, 11

A Solution Hey Ellie! Gosh! These guys can be so crazy and annoying sometimes huh?! They are probably just trying to fool you and play mind games with you. If you like one of them, try to go up to him or slip him a note asking what's going on and telling him how you feel. Maybe they like you and are too shy and embarrassed to admit it. Guys at age 11 usually don't know if they

HIKE ACROSS AMERICA FROM YOUR COMPUTER

Check out "On the American Trail." You can take a virtual hike through America. Get ideas for fun stuff to do outdoors together. Awesome!

http://www.altrec.com /features/ontheamericantrail/

What Other People Think

Sometimes it seems as if someone else's opinion of you is so crucial, you'll just despair if it isn't a good one. Really, some people who might feel very important at one time or another will leave you wondering "Do they like me?" which really means "Am I okay?" You know there are people who think you're great. Make a list of people who you want to think well of you. Start with your parents and include friends, teachers, neighbors, coaches, and yeah, maybe even a boyfriend. But at the end of it, remember this: It doesn't matter what boys think of you. What matters is what YOU think of them.

like girls or still think they are "gross." I don't see why they wouldn't like you, though! You seem like a sweet girl! Guys can be so weird at times, yet we girls still happen to fall for them! Hope I could help you, Ellie! Good Luck!!

—Trish, 13, Louisiana

Don't Want to Go with Him.

The Problem Dear Boy-Zone: What if a guy asked you out and you said yes because you were so shocked and you didn't want to hurt his feelings. Now you don't want to go with him. You have only a few weeks to decide. What would you do?

—Laura, 12

WAITING FOR HIM TO CALL?

Find out about your dog's personality.

http://www.dogskool.com/web /news/winter2000/page3.html

A Solution Hey, Laura! I would tell him the truth in a kind way. It is hard to do, but the right thing to do is to be honest and faithful to him. It might even make your relationship grow. Try it and see how it works. You never know. You might want to go out with him in the future. Things may work out between the two of you!

—Sarah, 15, New York

Saying "No" Gracefully

We've all done it—agreed to something we had no in-
tention of agreeing with. Saying yes too often, mostly
out of a desire to please everyone, can only backfire.
When you discover that tomorrow is Saturday, and
then realize you've agreed to help decorate the home-
coming float, clean the garage with your dad, babysit
for the neighbors, and go to the movies with your
friends—all at the same time!—you need to learn to
say no, and say it nicely. Try keeping a date book so
you can track when you've already committed to something. And when someone asks you to do or go or be
and you don't want to, or you're busy, just say no, I'm
sorry, but no. If you want, suggest another time or another activity. But saying no with grace is a skill that
will help you for the rest of your life.

Now draw a picture of yourself saying no. Write next to
it all the things you wish you'd said no to this year. You
go, girl!

Older Guy Leaves Me Cold, But He's My Bro's Best Friend!

The Problem Dear Boy-Zone: There is a guy who likes me, but I don't really like him. He's four years older than I am and is good friends with my brother. What is a good way to let him know I'm not into him without seeming, well, lame or hurting my brother's feelings?

—Suzi, 15

A Solution Hey Suzi! You're not lame for turning ANYBODY down, as long as you do so in a respectful way. Let him know that he's a nice guy but you just don't have feelings for him, and he's a little too old for you.

(*Editor's note:* It's better not to just pretend you already have a boyfriend because this older guy might just hang around hoping you'll "break up.")

Be mature about it (remember, you're dealing with a 19-year-old!), and he'll understand. As for your brother,

SHARE A SPECIAL MOMENT

Make a pineapple smoothie!

What you'll need: 2 slices of pineapple, sugar, a nice glass, 2 straws, a small cardboard heart (red or pink), 1/2 cup of water.

How to make it: Cut the 2 slices of pineapple into pieces. Put the pieces in a blender. Add 3 teaspoons of sugar and the water to the blender. Push the button that says "blend." WARNING: Do not put your hand inside the blender while blending; you can lose your hand or a finger! Start the blender until the mixture is foamy and smooth. Put it in a nice glass. Put 2 straws in the glass. If missing a little more sweetness, add more sugar. Cut a small groove at the bottom of the heart. Attach it to the edge of the glass. Add ice if you want it cold. Invite your crush over for a sweet as love pineapple smoothie! ;)

—Julieta, 12, El Salvador

he can't make it work between the two of you, so it's a pity for him, but don't let him force you into anything. Tell him nicely that you are flattered that he'd want his good buddy dating you, but you need to find your own guys, so you're letting him "off the hook" as your matchmaker!

—Tamira, 15, Belgium

My Vacation Romance Followed Me Home!

You Can Quote Me On That

I don't care who you are,
Where you're from,
What you did,
As long as you love me.
—From a Backstreet Boys song,
"As Long As You Love Me"
Submitted by
Julie, 14, Queensland

The Problem   Dear Boy-Zone: I just got back from a great holiday (vacation) where I met a really lush guy. We had a mini-romance (nothing serious). He is French. I can't believe it, but now he's here, and he thinks we are an "item." I never let him think I loved him. We only kissed a few times. Now I can't get rid of him. What do I do?

—Denise, 16

A Solution   Hey Denise! Wow, looks like you got a vacation AND a guy!!! Well, if that's how you feel, then the only way is to let him know. Don't try to ditch him or hide from him or anything. Don't call him, and if he asks why, tell him you're sorry if he thought you loved him, but you never felt that way.

Just kissing doesn't necessarily mean that you guys should be together forever. So let him know (gently) that you are not ready for a commitment or whatever he wants from you that you don't want. The only way I see out of this mess is one-to-one conversation. Go for it and good luck!!!

—Angie, 14, Washington

CHECK OUT MTV'S REAL WORLD PERSONALITY QUIZ

Have fun finding out which stars on *Real World* you two resemble!

http://www.mtv.com/mtv/tube scan/rw8/quiz/index.html

He Thinks I Only Pity Him.

The Problem Dear Boy-Zone: There's a boy in my grade who was in some sort of motorcycle accident; I don't know the specifics, but he has this scarred and morphed face. One day he admitted that he liked me. I tried to get him to go on a date with me, but he said

The art of love is largely the art of persistence.

—Unknown
Submitted by
Ashley, 15, Texas

that I was just trying to be nice and that I didn't really want to go out with him because of his face. But I really do like him. What do I say to convince him?

—Juliana, 15, Hawaii

A Solution

Hi Juliana! Personality is the most important thing, and you need to explain this to this guy. Say looks aren't very important when it comes to relationships. Why would you ask to take him on a "pity" date anyway? Explain that you don't go out with people just because you feel sorry for them. If you need to, tell him how much you like him.

This boy is probably feeling looked down on just now, so if you convince him to go out with you, you need to treat him like an equal, which is what he is. This will hopefully help him realize that it's what's inside that counts and that you're not "just being nice!"

> **"You Can Quote Me on That"**
>
> *If you judge people, you have no time to love them.*
> —Mother Teresa
> Submitted by
> Eva, 14, Singapore

Editor's Note: It's extra hard in the teen years to be "scarred" physically, whether from a bad case of acne, an accident, or birth defect. Kids with less than "perfect" faces are often going to either be extra shy or compensate by being extra macho or pushy. Take this into consideration when you interact with kids like this, and do for them what they most want—to be treated like everybody else.

—Lauren, 14, Scotland

All the Girls Are Dissing My Guy Pal!

The Problem   Dear BoyZone: Guys need help too. My best boy buddy has a problem, and I don't know what to tell him. He says this one girl in his class is cute, smart, funny, and hot, but she doesn't know he's alive. At his school they have this thing that if a girl wears a boy's jacket it means they're going steady with them. The girl can't talk to another boy unless she removes the jacket. Well, this one girl told my bud that no one will ever wear his jacket because he's too ugly. He wants to prove her wrong, so what should he do?

—Jordana, 13

WEBwatch

THE DATING PATTERNS ANALYZER

Check out your relationships. Find out what REALLY makes you happy!

http://www.netstorm.net /~mauldin/dpa/dpa.html

A Solution   Hey Jordana! I feel so bad for your friend. It sounds like the girl who said that to him is really inconsiderate. First of all, there shouldn't be any rules where girls can't talk to boys if they are wearing another boy's jacket! I'll bet the boys are allowed to talk to other girls, though, even if they let some "special" girls wear their jackets, right? You should tell your friend to ignore all of them. In fact, I don't think any girl in his class would deserve to wear his jacket if they live by these stupid rules! If I were a guy and I was in the same situation, I'd only want to give my jacket to a girl who is sweet, nonjudgmental, and sensitive. It doesn't sound like any of the girls in his class are like that or they wouldn't treat him that way. What if you were to wear his jacket? Even if the two of you weren't really boyfriend and girl-friend . . . at least he could say that someone has his jacket, and maybe everyone would be nicer to him, although I wish that he wouldn't have to do what they do to be treated right.

A better idea: You should tell the girls at that school that the rule stinks. Just because they are going steady doesn't mean they can't even talk to male friends! You and your guy friend could start a new trend! I hope I helped a little.

—Rachael, 17, Florida

Q. My little sister flirts with all my boyfriends. What would you do if this happened to you?

—Anonymous, USA

1 I'd tell her to knock it off or I'd tell our parents.

Mostly disagree   Somewhat disagree   Somewhat agree   Mostly agree

2 I'd help her find a guy her own age.

Mostly disagree   Somewhat disagree   Somewhat agree   Mostly agree

3 I'd just laugh it off. Your boyfriends think it's "cute."

Mostly disagree   Somewhat disagree   Somewhat agree   Mostly agree

4 I'd tell our parents and ask them to convince her she's too young for a boyfriend.

Mostly disagree   Somewhat disagree   Somewhat agree   Mostly agree

5 I'd try to embarrass her in front of my boyfriends so she'll stop.

Mostly disagree   Somewhat disagree   Somewhat agree   Mostly agree

Get In on the Fun!

Like the book? Check out the Web site! Come, join the fun!

What People Are Saying About Us

USA TODAY, **featured as "Everything a Girl Could Want"**:
"Since 1996, the only free online magazine with daily, weekly, and monthly features written and edited by girls and teens."

Snipped from *The New York Times:*
"There are a few wonderful sites that present utterly absorbing, enjoyable and comparatively safe places for pre-teenage and teen-age girls. In fact, I'm convinced that, taken together, Web sites like the ones reviewed here—Girl Tech, Purple Moon, and A Girl's World—may just be the "killer app" for girls. . . . A Girl's World is run by a staff of volunteers, almost all of whom are girls

themselves. The result is an admirable, if unsophisti-
cated, ezine for girls (that is an) amazing testament to
the creative energy of its visitors. . . . Although the
presentation of A Girl's World is simple and straight-
forward—nearly everything is rendered in text—it has
a greater abundance of spirit than a Girl Scout cookout
. . . refreshing."

**Snipped from Spun Gold Award for Excellence from
Kid's Domain:**
"This is a wonderful site for girls, with great content.
Any girl who wants to can submit an article, and get
credit for it! They will also receive a free year's member-
ship to Gold Key Circle and the safety measures (in a
Gold Key) are exemplary. There is no advertising, no
hidden agenda, just girls having fun!

"I simply can't praise this site enough! I couldn't find one
thing I didn't like about it, and I am pretty picky about
what I let my girls do and see. I have never been crazy
about the idea of kids chat rooms, either, but I like the
idea of the membership, password protected chat
rooms. . . . The articles are well-written and informative,
the crafts are fun, the teen advice column is right on target
with teen concerns, and being able to contribute your
own articles is a wonderful idea! A Girl's World Online
Club is definitely deserving of our Gold Award for
Excellence."

Snipped from the *Los Angeles Times,* **reviewed by
www.4kids.org:**
"A Girl's World Online Clubhouse is an incredible online
experience just for girls. As 'the space where girls rule the
place,' this monthly magazine is for girls of the 90s.
There is so much you could do, you could stay for days.
Make new friends, get to know women with dynamite

careers, find directions for neat stuff you can make and lots more! Girls are in the clubhouse, waiting for you to come share your thoughts on a million different subjects. So go, girl, and have a blast at the place 'where it's cool to be a girl!'"

What Girls Say About AGW

"This place rules!! I spend like 20 hours on here a month!"

—Jen

"I think it's awesome that people like you guys could start something like this. It's cool, and safe, just what on-line girlz need. KEEP UP THE GOOD WORK!"

—Shelley

"The Penpal program is great! And I LOVE the Baby-sitting classes! That's why it's a big thing 4 me. (The teacher's) doing a GREAT job! GIRLS' WORLD RULES!! Love,"

—Melissa

"I think the club is great. I pop in to the page every day when I get time."

—Aviva

"I got to talk to a real rocket scientist! I can't wait to tell all my friends. I love science. I want to be a scientist when I grow up."

—Holly

"This is one cool place for GIRLS where girls aren't expected to be wimps."

—Mallory

"When I first got here, I thought this would be all about makeup, prissy stuff like that. But it's not, so it's cool!"

—Samantha

"Hey! I just wanted to thank you for making this so fun. I am 15 and I am having lots of fun and was surprised to find people my age when I found this site. *THANKS ALOT!*"

—R DUDA

What Adults Say About AGW

"I recently had the pleasure of visiting AGW and was thrilled with what I found! It's such a pleasure to see a magazine for girls that doesn't dwell on "hot hunks" or how to increase your (physical) appeal. Girls of this age desperately need to be valued for who they are, not for how close they come to some Hollywood ideal . . . it's wonderful that you profile women of true achievement, not just models and actresses. Young girls need to have women to look up to, and you are doing a great job in providing role models."

— Kelly

"I very much believe in what you're doing for young girls. I think it's critical to have girl sites that don't just hawk the latest makeup trends, but that really promote independence and unique thinking. In any case, kudos to you for what you're doing. We need more young girls to have self-confidence."

—Heather I.

Awards

New members join every day, based on the recommendations of teachers, parents, and major search engines like Yahooligans, which rated us one of the "coolest" magazines on the Web for girls.

AGW was the first online site for girls recommended by CNN Interactive. Our Penpal Spectacular was cited by a major consumer reporting magazine. We've been awarded The Point's coveted "Top 5% of the Web" award and were cited as the best site on the Web for girls by the *San Diego Union Tribune*. We've been featured in other media, such as the *Los Angeles Times'* Cutting Edge, on KFI 640 am radio, and by *Family PC* magazine, along with numerous other awards.

We are recommended and listed by Sprint, Lycos, CNN, Prodigy Kids Pages, Cochran Kids Sites, Kidscom, About Me, 4Kids.org, Peekaboo, World Village, WWWomen.com, On Ramp-Canada, Femina, and Whidbey-Australia. Altogether about 1,400 other sites have created links to A Girl's World Online Clubhouse.

Use the Gold Key Chat Club to Meet New Friends

Give and get advice, get a pen pal without publishing your e-mail address, and do what you love to do—chat, meet great guests, post on message boards, play games, take our online class, and take our Babysitter's Certificate Class—all for free! It's a cool deal, a whole year of chat! That's a $5.00 value— FREE for any girl who buys this book! So grab your parents and fill out this form to join the fun!

What Gold Key Is: Gold Key is a private, member-supported chat club just for girls and teens the world over, ages 7–17. For information about what this members-only chatclub is all about, go here:

http://www.agirlsworld.com/clubgirl/gold-key/chatworks.html

Privacy and Information Use Policy: A Girl's World Online Clubhouse does not rent, sell, or give out e-mail addresses, addresses, mailing lists, or personally identifiable information about girls to anyone else. Ever. Period. All information on this form is kept strictly private and is used solely for signup, security, and contact information. We will not provide this information to any third party.

This signed permission form will complete your daughter's application. We will create a Gold Key Chat Club user name for her and mark her account as "paid" with full access for one year just as soon as this signed permission form is received. Thank you for helping us provide a safe, fun chat area for girls on the Web!

Problems? Get Help!

It can take up to a week after we receive your signed permission form to give your daughter access to the chat club. If you don't hear from us within 10 days, please do the following: First: Send a message to: lost-gk-pass@agirlsworld.com. The computer will let you know if we have a Gold Key user name for your daughter. If you get back an e-mail that says "no user name" and you sent in your form, please send an e-mail describing the problem to gk-problems@agirlsworld.com and we will check it out.

Thanks again to Prima Publishing and their support in making this the place where girls and teens rule the Web!

A Girl's World Gold Key Circle
Chat Club Membership Form

I, (Parent's Name) _____ certify
that I am the parent or legal guardian of (Daughter's Name)
_____, age _____.

I hereby give my permission for my daughter to participate in the Gold
Key Circle Chat Club. By signing up for and using this chatservice, my
daughter and I agree that we have read and agreed to follow these
chatclub rules at http://www.agirlsworld.com/clubgirl/gold-key/rules
.html and Terms of Service at http://www.agirlsworld.com/clubgirl
/gold-key/terms.html. I understand that AGW reserves the right to
delete without warning or refund any member of the Gold Key Circle
Chat Club who violates the Chat Club rules or Terms of Service.

Signed:

(Parent's Signature) _____ Date _____

Passcode Contact Information: We'll send your daughter's Gold Key
passcode by e-mail to the e-mail address below.

E-mail address _____

If we're unable to complete your daughter's chatclub signup, our
club will send a postcard to your mailing address. We will not provide
this information to any third party.

Mailing address:

Street: _____ Apt./PO: _____

City: _____ State: _____ Zip Code: _____

Country (if not USA): _____

International Postal Code: _____

Finish Your Signup

- Parents, please tear out, fill out, and sign this form.
  No facsimiles, please.

- Don't forget to check to see that the e-mail address is filled out
  so we can complete your signup.

- Mail your completed form to:

A Girl's World Online Clubhouse
Attn: Prima Books: Free Chatclub/Penpals Offer
825 College Blvd. PBO 102-442
Oceanside, CA 92057

Meet the Editor

PHOTO BY CANDICE CLEARY

My name is Angela Marie Ortiz. I am 14 years old. I was born on August 26, 1986, in Oceanside, California. I have a mom, a dad, two brothers, and one sister. My mom's name is Anna and my dad's name is Ed. My role model is my mom because of all the nice things she does for me. The names of my brother's are David and Kevin. David is 18 years old and Kevin is 16 years old. My 12-year-old sister's name is Gina. I am in 9th grade. I would describe myself as nice, caring and honest.

For fun, I go to movies, hang out with friends, go to the mall, shop, and play soccer. Whenever I feel blue, I sit on my bed and while I read books, I listen to music. The most exciting thing I've ever done was meet LeAnn Rimes in 1997. Recently I got a Certificate of Appreciation because I helped develop a SpayNow game on the Internet with the North County Humane Society.

I first became a member of the AGW girlcrew in May of 1996. I am one of the original members. Many things have changed since our first year. When we just started out, we only had about 8 pages and not very many editors. Now we have more than 600 pages and 90 volunteer girl editors. We also have many more activities.

Being a member of the AGW girlcrew is fun, exciting, and a really great experience. I keep coming back to AGW because I like being with all of my friends. Being a member of the girl-crew means a lot to me because it makes me feel important and happy and I enjoy being there. The opportunity that I get as a member of the AGW girlcrew is that I get to be a leader. Also we think of the activities. In A Girl's World, all activities are done by the AGW girlcrew.

The biggest challenge writing this book was finding the right stories. I like the way my book is set up and how the chapters go. I also love the activities girls can do while they read the book.

I think it is important for girls to give each other advice because that way girls can learn from other girls' mistakes and not make their own mistakes.

My hopes and dreams are to continue to be a soccer player, go to college, and eventually get married and have kids. I like being a girl today because we can do anything we want to do. The only advice I can give to girls who want to be writers is to keep up the hard work and never give up your dream.

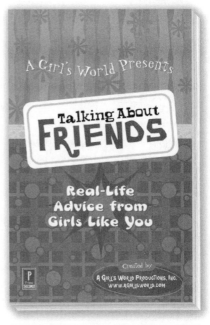

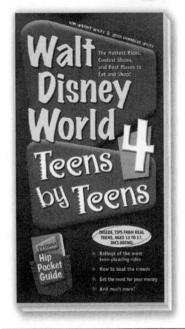